# WHO WERE THE PICTS?

This fascinating book deals with two subjects that have intrigued people for generations: Witchcraft and the Picts. Little is known about the Picts; however, this book is based on information taught by a descendant of these early Keltic peoples.

The Picts were eventually absorbed into what became Scotland, yet many of their individual traits and peculiarities have survived into the modern day. For example, the Picts were well-versed in herbal lore, both for medicinal purposes and as a means of survival in the wild Highlands in the north of Britain. This is one aspect of their Craft presented here. Their ways of divining—of looking into the future—are similarly included.

Witchcraft, far from being a dark, negatively-influenced path of malevolence, is in fact an extremely positive method of self-development and natural harmony. You will learn how *Wita*, or *Wicca*, ties in with the current ecology movement, and how Pictish Witans attune themselves to all aspects of nature: animal, vegetable, and mineral!

Along with the practical applications of Pictish Witchcraft are numerous tales culled from the folklore of Scotland, attesting to the old beliefs in spirits, gods, and magick. Traditional celebrations of the season are given, as are the reasons behind many of the age-old practices.

Through this book you will be able to understand the ancient ways but, perhaps more importantly, you will be able to practice these old magicks and become a part of the world of positive belief we call Wicca today.

# About the Author

Raymond Buckland has spent nearly half a century investigating various aspects of the occult, and has been active in Wicca, or modern-day white Witchcraft, for more than a quarter of a century. A protegé of the late Dr. Gerald Gardner, he was instrumental in introducing the Gardnerian branch of Wicca to the United States in the early 1960s. In the early 1970s he founded the Seax-Wica branch of the Old Religion and has since seen it spread and prosper. Contact with the late Aidan Breac led to his interest in Scottish Witchcraft and to writing this present volume.

Ray has written a large number of books, many of them now regarded as classics in their field. He has appeared both nationally and internationally on television and radio, and has spent many years lecturing and holding seminars across the country.

## To Write to the Author

We cannot guarantee that every letter written to the author can be answered, but all will be forwarded. Both the author and the publisher appreciate hearing from readers, learning of your enjoyment and benefit from this book. Llewellyn also publishes a bimonthly news magazine with news and reviews of practical esoteric studies and articles helpful to the student, and some readers' questions and comments to the author may be answered through this magazine's columns if permission to do so is included in the original letter. The author sometimes participates in seminars and workshops, and dates and places are announced in *The Llewellyn New Times*. To write to the author, or to ask a question, write to:

Raymond Buckland
c/o THE LLEWELLYN NEW TIMES
P.O. Box 64383-057, St. Paul, MN 55164-0383, U.S.A.

Please enclose a self-addressed, stamped envelope for reply, or $1.00 to cover costs.

Llewellyn's Modern Witchcraft Series

# Scottish Witchcraft

## The History & Magick of the Picts

Raymond Buckland

1992
Llewellyn Publications
St. Paul, Minnesota, U.S.A., 55164-0383

FIRST EDITION
Second Printing, 1992

**Cover Painting by Randy Asplund-Faith**
**Illustrations by Hrana Janto and Raymond Buckland**
**Photos by Gordon T. G. Hudson, Penny Yrigoyen**
   **and The Fortean Picture Library**
**Book and cover design by Terry Buske**


**Library of Congress Cataloging-in-Publication Data:**
   Buckland, Raymond.
      Scottish witchcraft : the history and magick of the Picts / by Raymond Buckland
      p.      cm.   (Llewellyn's world magic series)
      Includes bibliographical references.
      ISBN 0-87542-057.5 : $9.95
      1. Witchcraft—Scotland.   2. Picts—Religious life and customs.   I. Title.
      BF1581.B79   1991                                   91-32832
      133.4′3′09411—dc20                                  CIP




Llewellyn Publications
A Division of Llewellyn Worldwide, Ltd.
P.O. Box 64383, St. Paul, MN 55164-0383

# About Llewellyn's Modern Witchcraft Series

*Witchcraft* is a word derived from an older word, *Wicca* or *Wicce*. The older word means "to bend" or "wise." Thus, those who practiced Wicca were those who followed the path of the Wise. Those who practiced the craft of the Wicca were able to bend reality to their desires: they could do magic.

Today, Witchcraft is different from what it was eons ago. Witchcraft is no longer robes and secret rites. As the Aquarian Age—the New Age—approaches fruition, the mystical secrets of the past are being made public. The result is a set of spiritual and magical systems with which anyone can feel comfortable. Modern Witchcraft—Wicca—may be the path for you!

Llewellyn's Modern Witchcraft Series of books will not only present the secrets of the Craft of the Wise so that anyone can use them, but will also share successful techniques that are working for Witches throughout the world. This will include philosophies and techniques that at one time were considered foreign to "the Craft," but are now being incorporated by modern Wiccans into their beliefs and procedures.

However, the core of Wicca will stay the same—that is the nature of Witchcraft. All of the books in this series will be practical and easy to use. They will all show a love of nature and a love of the Goddess as well as respect for the Masculine Force. You will find that this series of books is deeply rooted in spirituality, peacefulness and love.

These books will focus on Wicca and Wiccans today, not what was done a hundred, a thousand or ten thousand years ago. They will help you to expand your horizons and achieve your goals. We invite you to follow this series and look toward the future of what some have called the fastest growing religion in the world, a religion that is personal, non-judgmental and non-institutional, natural and magical—that brings forth the experience of the sacredness of ALL Life. Witchcraft is called "the Old Religion" and it is found present in the oldest myths and artifacts of humanity. This series will help you see what it will develop into tomorrow.

## Other Books by the Author

*Practical Candleburning Rituals*
*Witchcraft From the Inside*
*Witchcraft ... the Religion*
*A Pocket Guide to the Supernatural*
*Witchcraft Ancient and Modern*
*Here is the Occult*
*The Tree: Complete Book of Witchcraft*
*The Magick of Chant-O-Matics*
*Anatomy of the Occult*
*Practical Color Magick*
*Buckland's Complete Book of Witchcraft*
*Buckland's Gypsy Fortunetelling Deck*
*Secrets of Gypsy Fortunetelling*
*Secrets of Gypsy Love Magick*
*Secrets of Gypsy Dream Reading*

with Hereward Carrington
*Amazing Secrets of the Psychic World*
with Kathleen Binger
*The Book of African Divination*
under the pseudonym "Tony Earll"
*Mu Revealed*

## Video

*Witchcraft Yesterday and Today*

## Forthcoming

*Ray Buckland's Magick Cauldron*
*Gypsy Shamanism*

*For Cecil Williamson, and*
*to the memory of Aidan Breac (1897-1989)*

# Contents

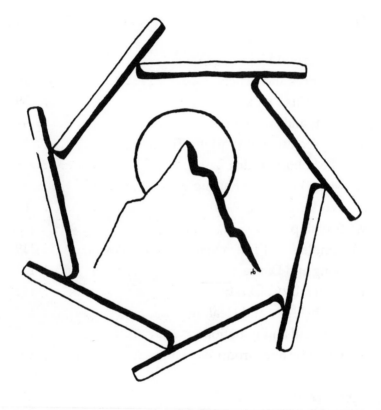

# Introduction

Witchcraft, or Wicca, is something which one *lives*. By that I mean it is not just something to do on certain occasions. Many followers of more traditional religions go to their places of worship just one day a week, and feel that this takes care of all their spiritual needs. And perhaps, for them, it does. But I have always felt that one should live one's beliefs twenty-four hours a day, seven days a week. I think most Wiccans feel as I do.

The problem, for many, is *finding* that "way of life" which is exactly right; the way that *can* be lived totally. When I wrote my *Buckland's Complete Book of Witchcraft* (Llewellyn, 1986) I included in it references to the teachings of Aidan Breac. Aidan was a Scottish Highlander who was born and raised in a hereditary Craft family on an island off the northwest coast of Scotland. He was descended from the Carnonacae tribe of Picts who lived in the northwest of what is now Ross and Cromarty County. For the last thirty years of his life Aidan devoted his time to teaching the PectiWita tradition. This book is written in response to the many people who wrote to me asking for more information on this Scottish tradition of the Craft.

My dedication of this book is to Aidan Breac, and also to Cecil Williamson. To my mind Cecil has never received the recognition he deserves. He was the founder of the Folklore Centre of Superstition and Witchcraft, on the Isle of Man, back in 1951; an organization to distribute facts on Witchcraft. He housed the Centre in the old Witches' Mill, on Arbory Street. In 1952 Cecil sold the mill to Gerald Gardner, who established his museum in it. Cecil has always maintained an interest in what he terms the "ordinary" Witch—the solitary practitioner who works magick when necessary and for whom the craft is a part of everyday life.

I hope that this present work will aid those seeking guidance along the Solitary path. There has certainly been very little written for the Solitary practitioner, other than Scott Cunningham's book *Wicca*, and small sections in books primarily devoted to coven work.

One of the interesting things about the Scottish PectiWita tradition, to me, is the fact that it is closer to what Cecil Williamson has always found: there is little emphasis on the worship of the gods (though it *is* there), but more on the living and blending of magick into everyday life. It seems to make Wicca, or Wita, a natural way of life, rather than just something one does on special occasions.

—Raymond Buckland
San Diego, California

# 1. Background

he Highlands of what is now Scotland were earlier inhabited by a people known as the Picts, or Pechts. In fact, this area was then known as "Pictland" and did not become "Scotland" until as late as the eleventh century. A second century Roman geographer, Ptolemey, drew the earliest known map of the region. On it he showed four tribes: the Venicones, Tazali, Vacomagi and Caledoni. By the third century these four had become two tribes, the Caledoni and the Maeatae, and by the end of the third century merged as one nation, the Picts.

The Picts have long been a mystery. One reason is that they spoke what is now a lost language, perhaps derived from the language spoken by the natives of the late Bronze Age in eastern Scotland. Like other lost languages of ancient Europe (*e.g.* Etruscan, Minoan), Pictish has disappeared by historical accident. When the Scots became the dominant force in the welding together of medieval Scotland, it was not in their interests to keep alive any Pictish traditions.

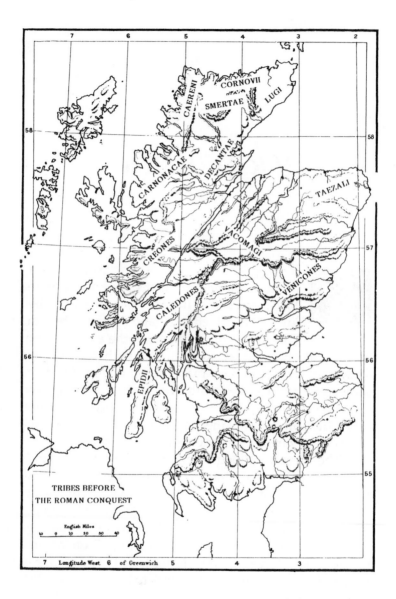

*Tribes before the Roman Conquest*

The Scots, incidentally, were immigrants from Ireland who, having come first as raiders, by the fifth century had settled in the under-populated areas of the west. By the seventh century they were virtually masters of the Lowlands.

## *LANGUAGE*

The common Keltic branch of language is divided into "Q-Keltic" and "P-Keltic." Q-Keltic is distinguished by the fact that it preserves the original Indo-European *qu* unaltered, whereas P-Keltic has turned this into *p* (a change that also took place in some Greek dialects). The Q-Keltic group is represented by the *Goedelic* (or *Goidelic*) languages; *i.e.* Irish, Scottish, Gaelic, and Manx, as well as in the hypothetical ancestor sub-dialect of common Keltic from which all descended. The P-Keltic covers a wide conglomeration of dialects including the Gaulish of Gaul, the British of Roman Britain, and the offspring of British: Welsh, Cornish, and Breton. These are all called *Brythonic* (or *Brittonic*).

Now, where does Pictish fit in? Was it a Keltic language and, if so, was it Goedelic or Brythonic or an independent off-shoot from the Gallo-Brythonic stage? Was it sister to Irish and Scottish Gaelic and Manx, or perhaps an archaic form of the Scottish? No one knows for sure. Apparently when Columba, the Irish missionary, visited Pictland in 563 C.E., he found it necessary to use an interpreter, so it obviously was not the same as Irish Gaelic, though it is usually assumed to be in the Geodelic family.

What of the Picts themselves? From various writers we hear that they dwelled in "waterless mountains"; that they had neither forts nor cities. They were pastoral and were hunters. Naked and unshod, the men frequently had wives in common, and the women husbands in common.

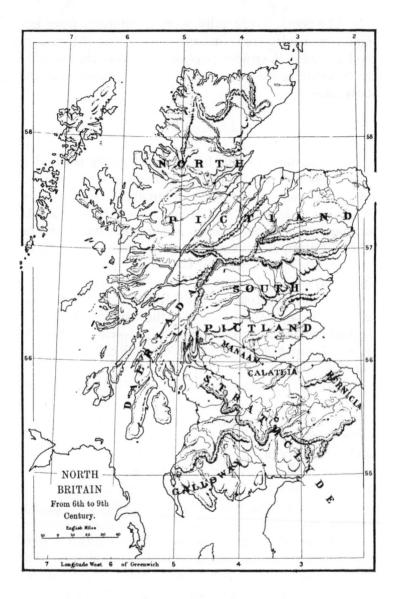

*North Britain—6th to 9th Century*

They fought from chariots; their horses were small and fleet. They themselves were small in stature and very swift. They frequently tattooed themselves with designs representing beasts (tribal markings?). Their weapons were *targe* (a small, round shield), dirk, and short spear or staff. Their dwellings were huts, frequently partly sunk into the ground and covered with sod, to give the outward appearance of small hills. Herodian said they were naked, with collars of iron or brass (torques). He also said that if a man were being sought, he could hide for days in a bog with only his head above the surface.

The Picts possessed a fleet of considerable strength, had skills in navigation, and dominated the Orkneys. The Pictish skiffs were large, open boats with twenty oars on each side. The boats and their sails were painted and dyed in a neutral color. In the middle of the sixth century the Pictish capital was at Inverness. King Brude lived in his palace on the banks of Loch Ness. In the ninth century (about 843 C.E.), the Picts and Scots were united under King Kenneth MacAlpin (*Mac Ailpein*), whose mother was a Pict.

## NORTH AND SOUTH PICTS

The Picts basically occupied the country to the north of the Firths of Forth and Clyde, with the exception of Argylshire. They were themselves divided into the Northern and Southern Picts—the latter occupied the territory corresponding to the counties of Perth, Fife, Forfar, and Kincardine. At different periods there were separate kings of the two, though at one time just one king ruled both sections and even had extended sway to the Orkney Islands. As in the case of Ireland, the country was probably divided into provinces. It was also subdivided among a series of greater and lesser tribes, who acknowledged the king, or kings, who in turn made good their sovereignty.

Apparently the Picts colonized Orkney and Shetland. Two sections of the Picts were called the *Orcs* ("Young Boars") and the *Cats*. Orkney was known as *Inse Orcc* ("Isle of Boars") and Shetland as *Inse Catt* ("Isle of Cats"). F. Marian McNeill (*The Silver Bough*, 1956) suggests this is a trace of totemism, with the clan or tribal names of the Picts, a suggestion also put forward by W. J. Watson (*Celtic Place Names of Scotland*) and Gordon Childe (*Prehistory of Scotland*). The people of Caithness (Cat-ness) and of Sutherland are still known, in Gaelic, as the *catach*, and the Duke of Sutherland is *Dinc Chat* ("Duke of the Cats"). In the Irish *Book of Ballymote* it is stated that "Cairneach was for seven years in the sovereignty of Britons and Cats and Orcs and Saxons."

As F. T. Wainwright says (*The Problem Of the Picts*, 1980):

> It would be a mistake to regard the Picts as remote and isolated barbarians; they had cultural contacts with Iona and Northumbria, and their kings were men of power and substance.

The right of succession to the throne was matrilinear—in other words, reckoned through the mother. This we know from one of the few extant documents of the period, the *Pictish Chronicles*, though this is little more than a list of the Pictish Kings. The practice of matrilinear system was in existence for well over three hundred years, that we know of, and probably much longer.

Most of the information we have about Pictish life and culture has been obtained through study of Pictish art, of which there are many examples in excellent condition. This art is characterized by the use of powerful

*Hilton of Cadboll Stone*

*The Rossie Stone*

*The Alberlemno Stone*

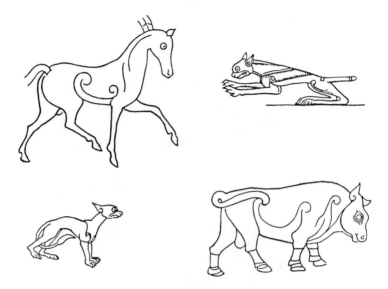

*Pictish Animals from various Scottish Stones*

animal symbols and geometric forms. Jewelry, metal-work, stone carvings; all show the same highly skilled craftsmanship. Apart from a few mythological beasts, the animals depicted in Pictish art are those found in every-day life and are easily identifiable. Pictish art gradually progressed from the early crude symbols carved on un-dressed stone (as at Inveravon, Inverurie, and Rhynie) to the very elaborate, smoothly done symbols (such as on Rodney's Stone at Brodie Castle) including battle and hunting scenes.

## *DRUIDISM*

"Before the coming of Christianity," says McNeill:

> . . .the religion of Scotland was Druidism, a form
> of sun-worship peculiar to the Celtic peoples. Like
> all sun-cults, it was based upon a universal doctrine
> regarding the two states of existence—the one in
> the visible world where the Sun-god reigns by day,
> and the other in the invisible or lower world into
> which he disappears at night, the relation between
> light and darkness symbolizing the relation between
> life and death. This concept is the basis of all the
> Mysteries.
>
> "Although the Order of Druids was probably a
> Celtic institution, Druidism itself appears to have
> been the aboriginal faith of Britain, its basic princi-
> ples being adopted by the Celtic invaders, who
> grafted it upon their own mythology."

Although we know very little of the details of the
Druids of Scotland, McNeill goes on to say that she feels it
certain they held a position of great authority:

> The names of many of them survive—Cathbadh, for
> instance, the Druid of Conchobar MacNessa and the
> instructor of Cuchulain; Abaris, a hyperborean Arch-
> Druid, who visited Athens in or about 350 A.D. on a
> diplomatic mission; . . . and Broichan, Chief Druid of
> the Court of King Brude, whom St. Columba encoun-
> tered at Inverness in 565.

Sir Thomas Innes of Learney (*Scots Heraldry*) traces a
Druidic line right through to the present, with the Lord
Lyon King of Arms:

> Each tribe had its own Druids, respectively priest,
> *sennachie*, and dempster or judge of the tribe, but
> the Druids regarded themselves as an Order and

*Typical British Druid*

Hierarchy, and just as the chiefs formed a nominal group under their Ardrigh, so the Druids appear to have been organized in what one might call a hierarchy or college, evidently under the presidency of the Chief Druid of the Pictish High King...The bardic and sennachiedal branch survived (the advent of Christianity) in two forms: (a) the Royal Heralds; (b) the tribal bards. It would be difficult to say that the second of these is even yet extinguished. They subsisted in many of the greater clans down to the middle of the eighteenth century. The office of Righ-sennachie...passed down into the 'Principal Herald' of our medieval history, for heraldry, as pertaining to the sennachiedal office, was added to his duties, so that the chief of the sennachiedal branch of the Druids evolved into the Lord Lyon King of Arms, whose brethren heralds, pursuivants, and macers, comprising the college of seventeen individuals, preserved the form of the primitive bardic incorporation.

Sir Thomas goes on to elaborate on the connection between the modern day Lord Lyon King of Arms and the ancient Chief Druid to the King:

Much of the Lord Lyon's peculiar importance in Scotland is due to his incorporating the pre-heraldic Celtic office of Chief *Sennachie* of the Royal Line of Scotland, ...his certification was requisite for the coronation of each Scottish king—whose genealogy it was his duty at each coronation as 'Official Inaugurator' to declaim in Gaelic—latterly for seven generations, but originally through all the Scottish kings back to Fergus Mac Earc, founder of the Royal Line.
...In ceremonial matters and grants of honour, Lyon's function can also be traced to origins only explainable by reference to the Sennachie's position as a *pagan priest*, and the primitive principle that it was *geiss* (taboo) for a king to speak in the presence of his Druid...Lyon thus appears in Scots history, not as a medieval invention, but with all the authority attaching to an ancient institution of the Celto-Pictish

regime, in which he exercised high administerial functions, sacred in the ante-Christian era, and subsequently of secular importance in a country where succession and civil rights depended on Patriarchal principles.

As Sir Thomas says, the ancient office of High Sennachie might have slipped into oblivion had it not been for the rise of medieval 'Chivalry.' For in Scotland there was already the keeper of genealogies, complete with full court and judicial status. He became "King of Arms of Scotland" and:

> . . . like other kings of arms, was endowed with the Sovereign's tabard, though the judico-priestly robe has continued, emphasizing Lyon's pre-heraldic functions as a judge and officer of state. In accordance with chivalric practice he was named after his Sovereign's 'beast.'

It is noteworthy that the Lord Lyon's two special courts are held on May 6 and November 6, which McNeill says are "dates which approximate to those of the two principle Druidic festivals and retain their names—the Beltane and the Samhuinn court."

## WITCHCRAFT AND MAGICK

Witchcraft was practiced in Scotland from earliest times. During the reign of Natholocus, in the second century, there was a famous Witch living on the island of Iona (a tiny island off the coast of the large island of Mull, in the Hebrides, off the west coast of Scotland). Such was her renown that the king sent a trusted messenger to her to find out what was going to be the result of a rebellion then building in his kingdom. The Witch said that the king would soon be murdered, not by an enemy but by one of his most trusted friends. When the messenger demanded to know the murderer's name, she said that he, the messenger, was the one. After much heart-searching, rather than return and report what the Witch had said, and perhaps be killed by the king in anticipation, the messenger did in fact stab the king to death.

There are many cases of Witchcraft throughout Scottish history, reflecting the bitter crusade pursued by Protestants and Catholics alike, in their paranoia over possible "servants of the Devil." The Scottish Kirk recognized the religious origins of Witchcraft and therefore applied to it the same sort of congregational frame of reference found within the Kirk, seeking out covens, or "coventicles," of thirteen—a leader and followers. The trial of Bessie Dunlop (1576) showed such a group, as did Isobel Gowdie's (1662) and Janet Howat's (1666). Yet there were few others that showed such organization. The vast majority of Scottish Witches, like their Pictish forebears, practiced as Solitaries, only occasionally coming together for special celebrations. Witchcraft was first made legally punishable, in Scotland, by an Act passed by the Scottish Parliament, in the reign of Mary, in 1563.

In *The Songs Of the Hebrides* (Vol. III), Kenneth Macleod says:

> The responsible witches of Gaeldom were highly gifted women who won their place by force of character and by right of service. Each would fight the other, and sometimes all the others, in defence of parochial rights and privileges. Each, too, made full use of all the arts, whether conventional or unconventional, to bring the luck of milk to her own sheilings, or the luck of fish to her own shores. . . But (they) were racial as well as parochial patriots. If the kiltless armies sometimes wondered why the mist was so thick and the rock so unexpected in

Gaelic territory, there was a woman in a place called Moy who knew... Behind Gaeldom stood Gormshuil of Moy and Doideag of Mull and Laorag of Tiree and Maol-odhar of Kintyre and Luideag of the Bens and Corrag, daughter of Iain the Fair, and Cas a' Mhogain Riabhaich from Glencoe . . . One would cross many a ferry to see seven old crones dancing hand in hand their circular dance to the rhythm of a maddening tune.

Magick in general seems to have been prevalent throughout Scotland till a very late date (if it is not still alive and well!). In the pages of Adamnan it is said that St. Columba regarded the Druids of the area as powerful magicians. Many of these magicians were from noble houses (*e.g.* Lady Glamis, Lady Fowlis and Sir Lewis Bellenden) and exerted great influence, oftimes protecting groups of Witches. The Earl of Bothwell's influence with the Witches of Berwick is an excellent example.

Testimony at the many trials shows that the Witches were generally charged with the working of harmful magick. Certainly the earliest laws indicated that the crime lay not in Witchcraft *per se*, but in the blasphemy and impiety of believing in supernatural powers. However, this quickly changed (see Appendix C) and, as the flames of hysteria spread, people were charged with everything from curing someone of disease (considered interfering with the will of God and therefore the work of the Devil) to causing the death of a neighbor.

In the seventeenth century the Church of Scotland tried desperately to get rid of the remains of "Druidical superstition and sorcery." In the minutes of the Kirk Session Register of Slains is recorded an inquisition, made by the ministers and elders into the Druidical practices and places in the parish. Rev. James Rust, in *Druidism Exhumed* (1871), reports that "several persons were 'delayit' or summoned before the Kirk Session for practising pagan rites in connection with hallow fires and refusing to till the ancient Druidical fields—those dedicated spots to which people resorted for the working of charms and spells. There were no fewer than three places within the parish that were dedicated to the 'Good People', or fairies, and these, incidentally, remained uncultivated until the beginning of the nineteenth century."

There are records of bulls being sacrificed in the remoter Highlands and of oblations of milk being poured on the hills. Even to this day there are traces of the old Druidical reverence for the sun. Earth and salt are still placed on the breast of a corpse, "for the repose of soul and body."

Charles Godfrey Leland looks at the origins of the word "witch" in his *Gypsy Sorcery and Fortunetelling* (1891):

> "The English word *witch*, Anglo-Saxon *Wicca*, comes from a root implying wisdom..." (Skeat's *Etymological Dictionary* states). WITCH: Mediaeval English *wicche*, both masculine and feminine, a wizard, a witch. Anglo-Saxon *wicca*: masculine, *wicce*: feminine. *Wicca* is a corruption of *witga*, commonly used as a short form of *witega*, a prophet, seer, magician, or sorcerer. Anglo-Saxon *witan*, to see, allied to *witan*, to know. Similarly Icelandic *vitki*, a wizard, is from *vita*, to know. WIZARD, Norman-French *wischard*, the original Old French being *guiscart*: sagacious. Icelandic *vizkr*: clever, knowing; with French suffix *ard* as German *hart*: hard, strong. That is, wiz-ard: very wise. Wit and wisdom here are near allied to witchcraft, and thin partitions do the bounds divide.

The form of Witchcraft that we shall be dealing with extensively in this book is that which stems from the time of the Picts. The late Aidan Breac, a respected teacher and practitioner, termed it *PectiWita*, or "Pictish Witchcraft." From just how far back it comes it is impossible to say, but it is certain that it differs in many ways from the Wicca of England; of the Gardnerian, Keltic, Saxon, Alexandrian and other varieties.

See also, Appendix C – *Witchcraft . . . The Religion—A Brief History*.

# 2. Practices and Beliefs

n my previous books on the subject, I have repeatedly stressed that Witchcraft is a religion. It is the present-day form of the old, pre-Christian, pagan religion of the common people. Today more generally referred to as Wicca (the original Saxon word, meaning "wise one"), it is mostly practiced in groups, known as *covens*. Although there certainly are Solitaries, they seem to be far outnumbered by the group Wiccans.

In fact, in many Craft traditions today it is virtually impossible for the individual to worship or to work magick alone, as a solitary Witch. Membership in a coven is deemed mandatory. This view, however, is inconsistent with the early history and traditions of Witchcraft. The annals of the Witch-Hunters record the existence of a large number of solitary Witches during the "burning times." These practitioners often dwelt alone, in remote sections of the countryside, in order to follow their beliefs more freely. Although they didn't belong to a coven they were still regarded as true Witches, both by the Witch-Hunters and by their peers. In Scotland this situation was, and still is, very much the case.

In *Rowan Tree and Red Thread* (1949), Thomas Davidson says:

> ...the conversion to Christianity (in Scotland) was a slow and very long drawn-out process. By the middle of the seventeenth century the conversion was complete only in so far as it applied to the townspeople and upper classes. In the country, it made little impression on the minds of the peasantry, who continued to adhere to the old beliefs to which they were accustomed.

Throughout the Scottish countryside, people—solitaries, or family groups—"continued to adhere to the old beliefs to which they were accustomed"; continued the practice of Witchcraft, and usually without the formality of coven membership.

And not only was there an emphasis on solitary practice, but there was little, if any, emphasis on the religious aspects of the Craft, as found further south in England. So, with the PectiWita we find a form of the Craft which is both *Solitary* and *mainly magickal* (rather than religious).

## FAMILY DESCENT

There are innumerable homesteads and small farms scattered throughout the Scottish Highlands (and some of the Lowlands). Most of them have been there for hundreds of years. Many of them house families and individuals who tie-in their lives with the passing seasons and who believe in the ages-old magickal practices of their ancestors. To work magick, to use herbs to heal, to look into the future—these things are as natural and as much a part of everyday living to these people, as is watching television to most Americans!

In the countryside of England—especially in the West Country—there are many folk who still follow the old ways. Most of these people would never refer to themselves as "Witches," yet Witches is what they are, as can be seen from their beliefs and their magickal workings (perhaps for the crops) as well as from their communion with the "Old Gods of Nature." Likewise in Scotland, there are many who would never even think of themselves as the PectiWita . . . yet here again that is exactly what they are, judging from their practices and their beliefs. For the purposes of this book, then, we will refer to these Scottish "nature-workers" as PectiWita, even if they themselves might not recognise the term. Incidentally, in Scottish folktales witches and wizards are always friends of the people, evidently being regarded, from ancient times, as highly honorable.

## GODS OF THE PICTS

If there was no great religiosity to the PectiWita, what *were* their beliefs regarding the gods?

Traces of the old Druidic reverence for the sun still linger throughout Scotland. It was believed that both sun and moon could exert strong magickal influences. In this respect the moon was more powerful than the sun. Fragments of runes have been found (the *Carmina Gadelica*) that translate into prayers to the sun and the moon:

> Sùil Dhè mhóir,
> Sùil Dhè na glòir,
> Sùil Righ nan slògh,
> Sùil Righ nam beo,
>     Dòrtadh oirnne
>         Gach òil agus ial,
>     Dòrtadh oirnne

*Gu foill agus gu fial.*
*Glòir dhuit fhéin,*
  *A ghréin an àigh.*
*Glòir dhuit fhéin, a ghréin,*
  *A ghnùis Dhé nan dùl.*

The eye of the great God,
The eye of the God of Glory,
The eye of the King of Hosts,
The eye of the King of the Living,
  Pouring upon us,
    At each time and season,
  Pouring upon us,
    Gently and generously.
Glory to thee,
  Thou glorious sun,
Glory to thee, thou sun,
  Face of the God of Life!

*Ri faicinn domh na gealaich ùir,*
*Is dùth domh mo shuil a thogail.*
*Is dùth domh ma ghlùn a leagail,*
*Is dùth domh mo cheann a bhogadh,*
*Toir cliù dhuit féin, a ré nan iul,*
*Gum faca mi thù a rithist,*
*Gum faca mi a' ghealach ùr,*
*Ailleagan iùil na slighe.*
*Is iomadh neach a chaidh a null*
*Eadar ùine an dà ghealaich,*
*Ged tha mise a' mealtainn fuinn,*
*A ré nan ré's nam beannachd!*

When I see the new moon,
It becomes me to lift mine eye,
It becomes me to bend my knee,

*Cailleach*
Illustration by Hrana Janto

It becomes me to bow my head.
Giving thee praise, thou moon of guidance,
That I have seen thee again,
That I have seen the new moon,
The lovely leader of the way.
Many a one has passed beyond
In the time between the two moons,
Though I am still enjoying earth,
Thou moon of moons and of blessings!

According to Aidan Breac, the "Mother of All" was CAILLEACH: an old "hag" often depicted with the teeth of a wild bear, or with boar's tusks. She was reputed to be a great worker of spells. One superstition regarding Cailleach that is still adhered to in some parts of Scotland is that whomever is last to harvest his crops must look after Cailleach for the rest of the year. So the first farmer to finish harvesting will make a corn-dolly from the last of the grain. He will pass this on to the farmer next finishing who, in turn, will pass it on to the next to finish, and so on. The farmer who is the last to finish harvesting gets the corn-dolly and is thereby obligated to look after "the old woman" for the rest of the year.

Fragmentary accounts survive of how Cailleach created the earth, fashioning the hills and the lochs, the valleys and mountains. According to Lewis Spence, she is a lover of darkness and winter:

With her hammer she alternately splinters mountains, prevents the growth of grass, or raises storms. Numerous wild animals follow her, including deer, goats, wild boars. When one of her sons is thwarted in his love affairs by her, he transforms her into a mountain boulder looking over the sea, a form she retains during the summer. She is liberated again on the approach of winter. (*Encyclopedia of the Occult*, 1920)

*Gruagach*
Illustration by Hrana Janto

Cailleach has also been identified with SCOTIA, after whom Scotland was named. Another variation on the name is SKADI.

If there was a male deity who was especially acknowledged it was GRUAGACH. The name means "the long-haired one" and Lewis Spence suggests that he is a form of sun-god, his streaming hair representing the rays of the sun. In the Western Highlands Gruagach was placated by oblations of milk, which were poured into a hollow stone known as the *gruagach* stone. He was extremely handsome and was looked upon as a guardian of cattle and as a valiant warrior and a sorcerer. "In Tiree, Skye, and elsewhere, the tutelary spirit of both castle and cattlefold is called the *Gruagach*," says F. Marian McNeill:

> ...and in Skye, *Gruagach* stones, where libations were formerly left, are still pointed out. One of these is at Sleat, formerly the residence of the Lords of the Isles, and the Gruagach attached by tradition to the Castle is said to have been frequently seen in the vicinity of the stone.

Another major god was TARANIS, a thunder god. The Gaelic for Darnaway (in the county of Moray) is *Taranaich*, from *taran* or *tarnach*, meaning "thunder." Lachlan Shaw, the historian of Moray, says:

> There Jupiter-Taranis might have been anciently worshipped. Taranis was the name of a Pictish king, and is to be equated with Taranis, the thunder god.

In the Island of Lewis there was a sea-god named SHONEY who ensured good fishing. His festival coincided with *Samhuinn* (or All Hallow's Eve). At that time of year, at nightfall, a representative of the island would wade waist-deep into the ocean, carrying a model boat filled with ale. He would hold it high and shout thanks and requests to the god:

> Shoney, I give you this cup of ale,
> Hoping that you'll be so kind
> As to send us plenty of sea-ware
> For enriching our ground the ensuing year.

He then upended the boat and poured the ale into the sea.

Then there was the bald and ruddy-faced MUIREARTACH, or "Hag of the Sea." She has a dark, blue-grey face and protruding, jagged teeth. She has but one eye, which gleams from the center of her forehead. She is the mother of the western storms, also mother of the king of Lochlann, the underwater realm of Keltic myth.

FIONN was a legendary figure who has almost achieved the status of deity. He was a warrior, a magician and a poet; he was a destroyer of giants and monsters. His band of followers were known as the Feine.

The SLUAG (pronounced "Slooa") was the Host of the Unforgiven Dead and a most formidable fairy of the Highlands. OGMA, "the sun-faced," was a powerful warrior who, like Hercules, carried a large club. He was the inventor of the Ogham, or Bethluisnion, form of writing. His brother was OENGUS or ANGUS, a sun god. CAMULOS (or NEITH) corresponds to Ares or Mars, as a god of war and of storms.

## SPIRITS

There was a strong belief in earth and water spirits, of various types. Aidan Breac tells us that earth worship—the propitiation of earth spirits—was a prominent feature of Scottish paganism. Children would often be conceived on a special piece of earth or an earthen mound. Contracts would be made by the parties swearing over a ceremonial piece of turf. Special mounds were used for ceremonial purposes. Offerings would be made at standing stones and sacred areas. Libations would be poured onto the ground; not necessarily for any particular deity, just onto the ground for the ground itself, or for the earth spirits.

*Giants* were supposed to be scattered generally across Scotland, from the border counties to Orkney and Shetland. Near Kingussie, in Strathspey, is found the Great Cave of Lynchat. This was supposedly made by giants, in one single night. Red Etin is the name of one with three heads, who lived in Preston, Berwickshire. Other names of well-known giants of the Orkneys and Shetlands are Atla, Cubbie Roo, Sigger, and the two brothers from the island of Unst, Saxi and Herman.

*Kelpies* are found in various areas, especially in the Hebrides. These spirits are described as having human appearance but may take the form of horses. In this form, the kelpies tempt humans to ride them, then plunge into water with them, drowning them. They then eat the flesh of their victims. The most famous kelpy was the one of Fitful Head, Shetland.

*Brownies* are another familiar spirit form. They frequently operate in pairs, husband and wife. Two famous pairs are those from Glenlivel and from Delnabo. The latter apparently squabbled a great deal. There is a very helpful brownie, known locally as "Broonie" at Noltland Castle in the Orkneys. Broonie is said to have built roads and will look after boats, making sure they are safely anchored during storms.

*Mermaids* are found scattered along the northern coasts. In Orkney tradition they are really the lovely daughters of the Fin Folk; tall dark men who wear close-fitting silver scales. They lived in a realm under the sea, though they also cultivated farms on the dry land.

Sacred wells and lochs were also common. At Kirkden, in Angus, there is a well the water from which is said to cure all sores. On the Isle of St. Kilda are two wells—*Tobar nam buadh* ("the spring of virtues"), the waters of which will cure deafness, and *Tobar a' chleirich* ("the clerk's well")—which get covered with seawater twice a day yet never become brackish. The divinities there had to be propitiated with offerings of shells, pins, needles, pebbles, coins and rags. In the north end of Skye, beneath the towering cliffs of Quiraing, there is a conflux of pure, freshwater springs which form an elliptical pond which is

*Tobar Hirta St. Kilda*
© Hamish M. Brown/Janet & Colin Bord

*Cloutie Well, Munlochy*
© Dr. Elmer R. Gruber/Janet & Colin Bord

quite deep. This is known as Loch Sianta, or "Holy Lake." For generations the local natives have made offerings at this loch. Invalids of various types go there to bathe in, and drink, the waters. Numerous mental and physical ills are recorded as having been cured thereby.

On the first Sunday of May the well at *Creagag*, or Craigie, in Munlochy Bay, was believed to possess powerful charm against disease and black magick. For weeks at a time pilgrims would prepare to travel to Craigie. They would offer colored threads and pieces of cloth, which would be hung on bushes about the well. *Tobar Leac nam Fiann*, the "Well of the Fian Flagstone," in Jura, could cure every disease known. The patient had to leave in it a pin, needle, button, or similar article for the cure to take effect.

On Skye is found *Tobar an Torraidh*, the "Well of Fertility." Farmers would drive their barren cattle to this well, the waters of which would make them fertile. Many local women who were barren would also, secretly, visit the well.

Loch Maree, in Gairloch, Ross-shire, also has its sacred well. The mountains which surround Loch Maree are of great height and incredible beauty. The gigantic Slioch (*Sliabhach*), reaching to over four thousand feet, can be seen from as far away as the Northern Hebrides. All around the loch are wooded islets of various sizes, with about twenty-five of them clustering near the middle of the lake. The loch is the center of innumerable legends regarding brownies, waterhorses, kelpies, and the like. The largest island is *Eilean Maree* (named after a petty king who occupied the island at one time), which has a burial ground containing tombstones bearing inscriptions and heiroglyphical figures which cannot be deciphered. On the island is a sacred well into which lunatics are lowered headfirst, to be cured. All manner of other people also claim to be cured by its waters. All around the well are the

*Loch Maree*
© Hamish M. Brown/Janet & Colin Bord

usual oblations, this time in the form of coins of every description stuck into trees that grow out of the bank. Queen Victoria once made a pilgrimage to this particular well, and held a religious service beside it.

## GATEWAYS TO THE OTHERWORLD

In Scotland islands are regarded as gateways to the Otherworld, if not the location of the Otherworld itself. Located off the west and far northern coasts of Scotland, the Hebrides and the Orkneys each have special legends and attributes as sacred islands, particularly as locations of the Otherworld. According to the *Cuchullain Saga*, there was a school for warriors on the island of Skye, led by the

*Ring of Brogar*
© 1987 Penny Yrigoyen

*Circle Stone Callanish*
*Isle of Lewis (close-up)*
© 1986 Penny Yrigoyen

*Callanish Isle of Lewis*
*Stone Row North of Main Circle*
© 1986 Penny Yrigoyen

warrior-queen Scathach. Many other figures in legend, including Merlin, are associated with off-shore islands. The mysterious Fortune Isles, the archetype of this theme, were ruled by the priestess, or goddess, Morgen, who held all arts and sciences in control of herself and her nine sisters.

There are a number of stone circles scattered throughout Scotland, including on many of the islands: Callanish on the wild Atlantic coast of the Island of Lewis, the Standing Stones of Stennis in Orkney, and the Clava Circle near Inverness, for example. McNeill suggests that Callanish may have been the "winged hyperborean temple" to which there is more than one reference in the classics. She says:

> Its shape is unique, being that of a Celtic cross—that is, the shafts of the cross are intersected by a circle. In the centre of the circle is a chambered cairn.

By bringing the upper part of a single line of stones to bear on the top of the large stone in the centre of the circle, the apex of that stone coincides exactly with the Pole Star.

The Stones of Stennis are in two main groups: the Ring of Brogar, or Temple of the Sun, and the smaller Ring of Stennis, or Temple of the Moon.

According to McNeill courts were held at these sites on a regular basis well into historic times. Certainly in 1349 the Bishop of Aberdeen held a court at the Ring of Fiddes, and in 1380 the son of Robert II held such a court.

In addition to the many circles, there are also a large number of single Standing Stones, associated with gods, spirits, and fairies.

*Callanish Isle of Lewis*
© 1986 Penny Yrigoyen

## SOLITARY PRACTICE

The Witchcraft practice of the Picts was, as I have said, a solitary practice. Central to it is a sense of "at-one-ness" with the earth. With the majority of Wiccan and most pagan teachings there is found a similar emphasis on Nature-empathy but this is more important, more intense, in the PectiWita. It is a symbiotic relationship that is reasonably easy to understand in theory, but not so easy to put into practice. There are, therefore, exercises that PectiWita students perform to obtain the necessary close ties. We will examine these exercises in the next chapter.

# 3. PectiWita Practice

As ozone diminishes in the upper atmosphere, the earth receives more ultraviolet radiation, which promotes skin cancers and cataracts, and depresses the human immune system ... As more ultraviolet radiation penetrates the atmosphere, it will worsen these health effects, reduce crop yields and fish populations. It will affect the well-being of every person on the planet. *Worldwatch Paper 87*, The Worldwatch Institute.

here is, and has always been, an empathy with Nature for those within the Craft. For this reason, if no other, the ecology movement is of paramount importance to Wiccans. The earth is our home. To judge from history, the earth is capable of surviving just about anything we inflict upon it. But will *we* survive along with it? It seems unlikely. By pollution of air, earth and water, by industrial pollution and the dumping of toxic waste, by the destruction of the ozone through the continual use of chlorofluoro-carbons, carbon dioxide, methane, nitrous oxide and ozone, we seem destined to destroy life on earth as we know it and as we can be a part of it. We (speaking of humankind as a whole) refuse to listen to the many warnings from knowledgeable scientists and others and plunge onward toward our eventual demise. Oh, I am sure that eventually there will be a sudden final realization by "the authorities," and that vested interests will at last be ignored, with laws rushed through . . . but almost certainly it will be at a time that is far too late for humankind and for life as we have enjoyed it for the last several thousand years.

### AT-ONE-NESS WITH NATURE

In *British Calendar Customs* (Scotland), Mrs. MacLeod Banks says:

> Everywhere the earth itself or the power connected with it has commanded the reverence of man . . . As parent of life and controller of fate, it was seen to hold beneath its surface the secret of growth and renewal of the mystery of decay; it was, as we know, the centre of the most ancient faiths.

Ancient peoples of Scotland swore oaths by the earth. An insulted chief would pick up a piece of sod and, holding it over his head, shout "Vengeance!" Highland midwives gave newborn babies a small spoonful of earth as their first meal. Both salt and earth were placed on the chest of a corpse, as I mentioned in Chapter One. New laws were proclaimed from earth mounds. The courts of the Brehons (judges) were held on the side of a hill.

Happily, as I have said, most Wiccans are devout followers of earth conservation. Not just with the practicality of recycling newspapers, cans and bottles, but from the point of view of recognizing that humankind is, quite literally, a part of nature. Wiccans are the people who hug trees, who walk barefoot across plowed fields, who talk not just to animals but to plants and even minerals!

But where this is true of many Wiccans, I would venture to say it is true of *all* PectiWitans. Certainly the training of Aidan Breac focuses on this kinship with nature. In that sense it is a true shamanic path.

But how, you might ask, can I see myself related to, for example, a quartz crystal? As Jose and Lena Stevens put it, in *Secrets Of Shamanism* (1988):

> To the uninitiated and inexperienced the wind is the wind, a rock is a rock, and a tree is just a source of lumber or shade; water is for drinking and washing, animals are flesh-covered bones, and humans are flesh, blood, thoughts, and feelings. Take them apart and all you find are smaller pieces of them. Take them down to the atomic level and, surprise, they are all made of the same basic materials. Take them down to the subatomic level and, voilà, they are mostly space (or spirit). They are particles that are really waves or vice versa. At this level, chaos begins to reign for the physicist, but not for the shaman . . . From the shamanic point of view, there is spirit within all wind, within all rocks and earth, within all plants and trees, water, animals, humans, and every other form of life both animate and inanimate.

Yes, if you take us all down to the basest level, we are all the same.

We all may share in this common spirit; in what shamans think of as a "web of power" common to all. Through this web of power we may communicate one with another.

As part of PectiWitan training there is something akin to the Amerindian and other cultures' vision quests. But with the PectiWita it is not a case of trying to obtain an actual vision, of a guardian or a power animal, it is simply a quest to "make contact with the earth," as Breac puts it. The Witan will go out into the Highlands, camping and living off the land for several days, and try to attune him- or herself with the land and all that lives thereon (see Chapter Fourteen). Lives—of rabbits, fish and fowl—are taken but only after the Witan has "mind-melded" with the creature, as *Star Trek*'s Spock would say. There is recognition that humans are meat-eaters (and are far from unique in this, of course) but also acknowledgement that we must not kill for sport, only in order to eat when there is a need to eat. Breac has little time for vegetarians who cry out against the eating of meat solely on the grounds of it being "life." "We are all life," he says. "Humans, animals, plants, and even minerals." [He recommends such non-meat-eaters read *The Secret Life of Plants* by Peter Tompkins and Christopher Bird (New York, 1973) and *The Secret Power of Plants* by Brett L. Bolton (New York, 1974)]

On this seven-day sojourn the PectiWitan learns much; learns not only to understand nature but to merge with her. With no radio or television, the Witan comes to appreciate the music of the birds' songs, of the babbling burns, of the rustling leaves, of the wind across the mountain tops. By sleeping on the earth—lying on her—you pick up the heartbeat of nature. The breeze is a kiss and the warmth of the sun a caress. The soft splash of rain is a refreshing cleansing of the spirit as well as the body. This is the true initiation into the PectiWita tradition, and I will detail it in later chapters.

## STONES AND TREES

In *Earth Rites* (1982), Janet and Colin Bord suggest that the many phallic-shaped stones found across the length and breadth of Britain "were not only symbols, but actual tools, carefully placed for very good reasons...They may have actually been huge stone phal-luses, capable of accumulating natural energy and direct-ing it into the earth—impregnating and fertilizing the Earth Mother."

Certainly energies exist and are easily felt, by even the only-slightly-sensitive, at many of the sites of standing stones, such as at Stonehenge, the Rollright Stones, the Hurlers stone circle, the Merry Maidens, and the Pipers.

Yet it is not only ritually-positioned stones that con-tain energy. All stones have it. The Scottish "Stone of Scone" rests under the Coronation Chair in Westminster Abbey. Thirty-four Scottish kings, and every English monarch (except Queen Mary I) since Edward I stole the stone from Scotland in the thirteenth century, have been

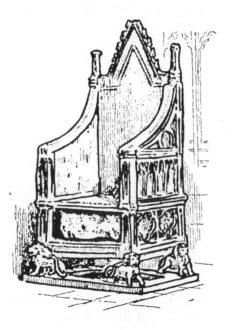

*Coronation Chair and the Stone of Scone*

crowned while seated upon it. It is believed to be a stone of great power. Legend identifies it with the *Lia-fail*, the coronation stone of the old kings of Ireland.

Douglas Hill (*Man, Myth and Magic*) suggests that the concepts of "the god-as-the-stone" and "the god-in-the-stone" frequently developed into a belief that a particular stone was a sacred object. "The presence of pebbles, ordinary stones and chunks of unhewn rock in so much mythical and magical lore reflects mankind's willingness to find the supernatural in anything and everything." Read the word "find" in the sense of "discover," and he has a point. The "supernatural"—or supranatural . . . transcending the boundaries of the ordinary, everyday—is in everything. Let's return to stones in particular.

Pick up a stone and hold it to your chest. Close your eyes and center yourself, breathing deeply and regularly. Allow your whole body to relax. Then blend with the rock. Feel its heartbeat . . . and after a while you *will* be able to sense it. Feel its strength and attune yourself with its special life force. All stones have a self-generating power that can be felt by the sensitive. Ofttimes this is a healing power, that can be used to advantage . . . and any time you use such energy—be it from a rock, tree, animal, or whatever—don't forget to give thanks for the use of that energy.

Francois Strachan says that trees are like radio transmitting stations, receiving and transmitting the vibrations in our natural universe. They are certainly generators. In his *Patterns In Comparative Religion* (1958), Mircea Eliade presents an in-depth study of cults around the world that have vegetation rituals and regard for the sacred nature of trees in particular. He talks of the tree "as symbol of life, of inexhaustible fertility, of absolute reality; as related to the Great Goddess or the symbolism of water; as identified with the fount of immortality."

Oaks and thorns were especially, though not exclusively, venerated throughout Britain. Many villages and small towns still preserve an ancient tree, and even still hold regular rituals and/or dances around it—Aston-on-Clun, Shropshire; Barnham Cross, Norfolk; Barwick, West Yorkshire; Padstow, Cornwall, for example.

I mentioned Witans hugging trees. Try it yourself. Choose a tree that is fairly old, to start with. Oaks are good, as are pines, but any tree will do. Stand with legs apart, feet flat on the ground (take off your shoes for better contact to the earth), and spread out your arms around the tree. Hug it. Close your eyes and flatten your cheek against the bark. Try to clear your mind of any special thoughts and leave it open for anything to come in. Again, as with the stone, you will become aware of the heartbeat within. Blend with it.

Trees have great healing energy. Sit with your back up against the tree. Stretch out your legs in front of you and lay your hands flat on the ground. Close your eyes and absorb the energies of the tree. If you were feeling at all tired, up-tight, angry, depressed, mentally or emotionally down, the tree will pick you up. You can be aware (and a PectiWitan should be aware) of the energy flowing from the tree into your body. For me it is a sense of warmth and, as the energy seeps in, a feeling almost of molasses being poured! You will experience a greater and greater feeling of wellbeing. Once again, when you have finished, when you feel sufficiently uplifted, turn and thank the tree with a hug.

With experience you will become aware of different energies and powers from different trees. Both from different species of trees and also from individual trees. Another way to recognize this is to stand with your arms stretched out in front of you and your palms flat on the trunk of the tree. In a woods, or with a small group of trees, try this, going from tree to tree. Spend at least five minutes with each tree. You will soon become aware of the differences.

## A LEARNING

So, through a prolonged journey, the Witan draws close to nature and comes to better understand that we are all one. Along with this attunement, Breac set the tasks of survival for the initiate. You must learn to make shelter, when needed; to make fire, to cook and keep warm; to kill and clean food. You must learn to recognize what nuts, fruits, herbs, fungi, and roots are edible. How to heal, if necessary, and to skry. How to speak with the gods and to work magick. All of these things we will be covering in this book.

# 4. Tools and Accessories

wide variety of "working tools" are found in Wicca. In the Gardnerian tradition, for example, there are eight such tools: Athame, Sword, Wand, White Handled Knife, Scourge, Cords, Pentacle and Censer. The Frosts-Celtic add an Egyptian Ankh and a Broom but leave out the White Handled Knife, Sword and Pentacle. The Sicilian tradition dispenses with Sword, Wand, Scourge and Pentacle. The Seax-Wica uses only a Knife (*Seax*), Spear and Sword. Different tools for different traditions; each using what it deems necessary and (presumably) *only* what is necessary . . . though in some Wiccan denominations—noticeably many "eclectic" ones—there is found a plethora of tools.

Throughout the Middle Ages there was a certain intercourse between Witches and Ceremonial Magicians. Witches, of course, were being badly persecuted at that time, and having to work in hiding. Magicians, on the other hand, could practice quite openly. The reason for this is that Witchcraft was recognized as a religion, and therefore a rival, by the Christian Church, whereas magick was viewed as simply a practice and therefore non-threatening. Indeed, many high clerics became frequent practitioners of Ceremonial Magick.

With this intercourse between Magicians and Witches it is only natural that there was an experimentation in one another's methods, eventually leading to adoption of useful tools. In this way, it is almost certain, such tools as the Wand, the Pentacle and White Handled Knife, came into Wicca. My personal feeling has long been that many of these adopted instruments were not really necessary and almost certainly were not found in Wicca in its very early days. Wicca was very much the religion of the ordinary, common people; those who were not even aware of things like "symbolic representation of the elements," and the like. They were the people who worked with the basics.

My feelings seem to be borne out with what we find in the PectiWita. As an extremely old, solitary tradition, its adherents work with the very minimum of tools. And these "working tools" are equally useful in everyday living; a fact which, in a sense, makes them especially sacred.

## STAFF

The first of the PectiWita tools is the *STAFF*. If you want to compare it to the tools of other traditions, it is the Sword and the Magick Wand both rolled into one. Obviously for the Highlander, traveling over mountainous regions, it is a useful, if not essential, piece of everyday equipment. It can even be used as a weapon, of defense or offense. But for the PectiWitan it is more than that. It can be used to mark and to consecrate a ritual Circle. It can be used to direct energy/power into that circle, or for the working of magick. Like the Wiccan's Athame, the PectiWitan's Staff is his or her personal tool; the one which is

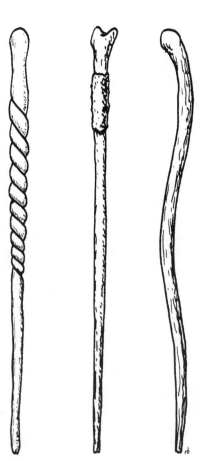

*Staffs*

most used, thereby absorbing most of the individual's energies. The Gaelic for "a magickal staff" is *an luirgean*, or *an lorg ohn*.

The Staff is usually of chest height, though I have seen those that are the same height as the owner. It is made of hard wood. Oak and yew are popular, as are walnut and ash. Thickness of the shaft should be simply what is comfortable to hold—probably about one-and-one-half inches in diameter, tapering down to roughly half of that. The staff need not be absolutely straight, from end to end. I have seen some with bends in them, some with twists, but the bottom one-third of it should be as straight as possible.

You should cut the staff in the *waxing* phase of the moon (after the new moon and before the full) and let it dry out thoroughly and slowly, at room temperature. Do not try to hurry things by fast-drying it. You may strip off the bark or leave it on, whichever you prefer. You could take off all of it except for a strip to act as a handgrip near the top. Alternatively, you may want to bind leather, or fur, around the staff for a handgrip.

The Staff may be left natural or stained/varnished/ oiled. You can even paint it, if you wish, though I have seen few that have been more than slightly "touched up" with paint. Yet most Staffs that I have seen have at least been slightly decorated, with a name carved or burned into the wood; with feathers or fur attached; with carvings or the embellishment of natural aberrations. Some PectiWitans actually name the Staff, and this name is carved or burned into it. When it comes to any form of writing, on this or any of the other tools, the PectiWitan Runes are used or, occasionally, the Pictish glyphs (see APPENDIX A), though these latter are not easy to work on wood.

## DIRK

The second PectiWita working tool is the *DIRK* (*Durk*). This is a long-bladed knife; typically with 11-3/4" long blade and being 17-1/4" overall. Often Dirks have beautifully decorated blades, engraved or etched with typical Scottish motifs such as thistles. Many of these can be bought at Scottish Highland Game festivals across the country, or from Scottish import stores. But again the "nicest" Dirks I have seen have been those that have been home-made and are more simply decorated, with carvings and etchings/engravings done by the maker. In my book *Buckland's Complete Book Of Witchcraft*, (Llewellyn, 1986) I give a method for making a knife, starting with base metal and working through the regular blacksmithing steps. You can follow these directions for making the Dirk. If the above mentioned dimensions seem too large for you, then modify to what seems more suitable. On the whole, however, PectiWitan Dirks are fairly long knives.

## KEEK-STANE

The third, and last, of the main PectiWita tools is the *KEEK-STANE*. This is, in effect, a skrying stone, or the equivalent of a crystal ball, though it is much easier to carry around than an actual ball would be. (As you will learn, there is a lot of divination done in PectiWita.)

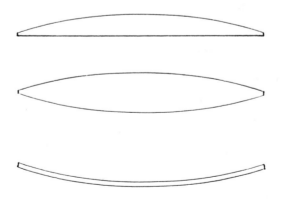

*Lenses*

The best thing for making a Keek-Stane is a non-magnifying clock glass. These are usually concave on one side and convex on the other. A good size for the lens is about three inches in diameter. They can be obtained from stores selling and servicing watches and clocks. They can also frequently be found in antique stores, swapmeets and thrift stores.

The glass should be carefully washed in warm, soapy water, rinsed in clear water, and then left to dry in the sun. The front (concave) of the lens should be left clear but the back (convex) is to be painted black. Use a good black enamel and give two or three coats. Make sure there are no brush strokes apparent.

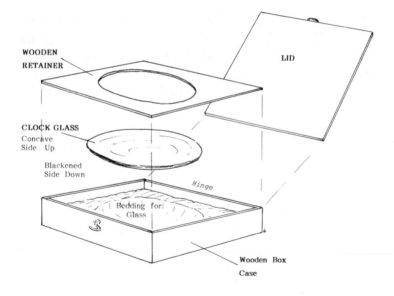

WOODEN
RETAINER

LID

CLOCK GLASS
Concave
Side Up

Blackened
Side Down

*Hinge*

Bedding for
Glass

Wooden Box
Case

*Keek Stane*

Old *grimoires* for Ceremonial Magick give recipes for the paint, using such items as turpentine followed by three coats of asphaltum. This was fine a few hundred years back, simply because a good black enamel wasn't available! But today, why not use what we have? The effect will be the same.

While waiting for your paint to dry, start work on the case for the Keek-Stane. You need a wooden, lidded box that will just hold the glass. You can fill the box with styrofoam, or similar, and then hollow out the center so that the glass will sit nicely in it. If you don't want to use such a modern material as styrofoam (and we should not encourage its use), then use rubber, particleboard, or pack it with wood shavings, or whatever. The idea is to have a bed on which the glass will rest flat and not tip. Then, on top of that, is placed and glued a flat top with a circular cut-out, to retain the glass yet allow you to see it. The diameter of the cut-out should, then, be just a little less than the diameter of the glass.

If you cannot get a good watch-glass, you could use a regular lens and have the top surface convex, but a concave gazing surface is definitely superior.

If you wish to carve or burn designs into the wood of the box, and/or around the stone itself (on the retaining piece of wood), that is fine, but it is not necessary. However, do stain the wood of the inside of the box a dark color, so that when you are gazing into the stone you are less likely to be distracted. The outside of the box can be decorated as you wish. I have even seen some decorated with silver, gold, copper, brass, jewels, etc., and with the inside of the lid lined with dark blue silk or velvet. Many have PectiWitan symbols engraved on the outside. Don't forget a catch of some sort to hold the lid closed, when not in use.

## ADDITIONAL PECTIWITAN TOOLS

The Staff, Dirk, and Keek-Stane are the three main tools of the PectiWita. There are then other "occasional" tools that might or might not be used, depending upon the individual and the circumstances.

*MOOL* – Earth, usually in an earthenware bowl. In some rituals a representation of earth is needed and in many Wiccan traditions salt is used as this representation. In the PectiWita they use the real thing (which seems to make more sense). *Mool* is used in the Sabbat rituals.

*QUAICH* – A cup. It can be of any type, though drinking horns that can be hung from the belt are popular. It may be used for everyday drinking but is usually reserved for occasions when it is felt necessary to pour libations to the gods, or similar ritual use.

*INCENSE* – Today there is found more use of incense per se, but it used to be that when there was felt a need to have incense the PectiWitan would burn something natural (as Amerindians burn sage). Favorites were Sweet Flag (*Acorus calamus*), Scotch Heather (*Calluna vulgaris*), Catnip (*Nepeta cataria*), Milfoil (or Yarrow, *Achillea millefolium*); and the resin excreted from Scotch pine trees. Wolf Claw (or staghorn, or foxtail, *Lycopodium clavatum*) was also sometimes burned for cleansing rituals. Sweet Flag was the favorite for burning to aid divination.

No actual incense-burner, or thurible, would generally be used, if incense was to be burned (though you certainly can use one if you wish). Rather, the PectiWitan would find a depression in a rock, or make one in the ground, and lay a glowing ember from the fire in it, then sprinkle the herb on that.

*BELL* – Some Witans use a Bell in their rituals, though not all. Certainly sound is vibration and vibrations are important, not only in everyday life but, especially, in magick. To help achieve the right vibration(s), the right "mood" or "frequency," it helps to ring a bell. It can actually be just as effective—and thereby as important—as the burning of incense, which also affects vibrations. Personally I always use a bell. Don't overdo the bell ringing. A very occasional single-, double- or triple-ring, scattered throughout a ritual, can be far more effective than a constant jangling.

The bell you use should be chosen carefully. Don't just take *any* bell—each has its own particular timbre. Find one which seems "right" for you, one which soothes and mellows rather than one which is harsh and strident. If possible, remove the handle and replace it with a leather loop. In this way you can carry the bell strung from your belt.

These are the only tools you are likely to need in the PectiWita. Others can certainly be added to individual taste, on occasion, but are really not necessary. A candle might well be burned after dark, when doing a ritual, but this is not considered a tool or even an altar essential—the Witan is just as likely to be working in the light from a fire. If you are working with herbs, pestle and mortar are almost certain to be used but, again, these are not regular ritual tools. So with anything else—tarot cards, pendula, cords, crystals—these are a matter of personal, occasional use only.

# 5. Consecration of Working Tools

OUR working tools need to be consecrated before they are used. Consecration is a ritual cleansing. In effect you are getting rid of any and all negative vibrations connected with the article and starting afresh in its use. Let us first look at the consecration of the Staff.

## STAFF

This ritual should be done at daybreak; in the first rays of the rising sun. The day of the week is unimportant, as is the time of the year. All that is important is that you can clearly see the rising sun.

The consecration of the Staff should be done on as high a piece of land as you can find. (If you live somewhere like Florida, an area with virtually no high ground, then do the best you can—you could perform the ritual in a room on the upper floor of a tall building, if you wish, though personally I feel that being outdoors is more important than the height factor.) Many of the PectiWita would climb to a mountain top just for this ritual. Aidan

*The consecration of the Staff should be done at daybreak,
in the first rays of the rising sun.*

Breac would insist that his students do just that, in fact
having them climb the local Ben the previous night and
camp up there awaiting daybreak.

Have a small fire alight beside you. Onto the fire,
throw some Wolf Claw (*Lycopodium clavatum*) and Common Nettle (*Urtica dioica*). If you are unable to obtain
these, or would prefer to use incense, then use Frankincense. Hold the Staff in the smoke of the burning herbs
and thoroughly cense it.

*Staff consecration—breathing life into it.*

Then turn and, facing East, stand holding the Staff upright in front of you. Breathe in and out deeply, a half dozen or so times, and feel the rays of the rising sun striking your body and filling it with golden light. Feel the light traveling down your arms and legs, into your hands and feet, and filling your whole body. Feel it driving out any impurities and filling you with its light and strength. Now hold up the Staff in front of you, as though it were a blowpipe, or a long musical instrument. Take another deep breath and blow "into" the (thick) end of the Staff. You are breathing life into it. Do this three times, blowing and sensing the golden sunlight flowing now from your body into the body of the Staff. Feel that you are literally giving your Staff the breath of life; that, as of this moment, it is a living thing.

Then take your Staff in both hands and hold it high, horizontally, above your head. Shout aloud:

*A null e; A nall e; Slàinte!*
Here is my brother/sister; my other self.
I give this Staff strength
To do all that I might require of it.
I name this Staff .....;*
Let it serve me in all ways I may use it!

[*A null e; A nall e; Slàinte!* can be translated as "Away from me; Towards me; Life/Health!" *Slàinte* is pronounced (roughly) "slansh"]

Bring the bottom end of the Staff down and pound it on the ground, saying:

---

* Many Witans name their Staff and their Dirk. This makes them much more personal. Here are some names taken from Pictish history, should you wish to use them: Bargoit, Bredei, Broichan, Brude, Derelei, Drosten, Emchat, Forcus, Kinpout, Lutrin, Nechton, Peanfahel, Pictus, Talorg, Uen, Urad.

Let this Staff be rooted in the earth!
Let it draw forth its strength from there,
Even as the trees and the plants draw theirs.

Keeping the base on the ground, swing the top of the Staff down at an angle, away from you, and move forward to sit astride it. Grasping it firmly, concentrate on the head of it. "See" the power from your body coming out from the Third Eye and entering the top of the Staff. See it as a stream of golden light being absorbed into the wood. See the energy filling the Staff with your personal power. Keep this up for several minutes, until you feel you have directed as much energy as you can, then stand again with your Staff in your right hand.

*The Crouch*

This is now your personal tool/weapon; your kin. Take good care of it and it will take good care of you.

## DIRK

The consecration of the Dirk should be done immediately following that of the Staff. Laying down the Staff, take out your Dirk and hold it in the smoke of the fire (throw on more Wolf Claw and Nettles if necessary), turning it so that it is thoroughly censed in the smoke. See the impurities leaving the knife. Then hold it high in your right hand (left if left-handed), in the light of the rising sun. Again feel the rays of the sun recharge your body. Take a number of deep breaths as the light flows in, filling you with its golden purity.

Now bring the Dirk down in front of your face and hold it with both hands. Do not, of course, look directly into the sun (at any point in these consecrations), but look towards it with the Dirk between your eyes and it. See the Dirk silhouetted against the brightness and picture the energy flowing in both directions—from the sun into the Dirk and from you (down your arms and hands) into the Dirk. Know that the knife is being cleansed and energized.

Reverse the Dirk, so that the blade is pointing down and, taking a deep breath, blow life into it through the base of its handle. Give three good "breaths of life." Then hold it high in your right hand again. Say:

A null e; a nall e; Slàinte!
Here is my Dirk;
My heart and my strength.
May it serve me well in all things.
Let it absorb the Energies of Light
And be as powerful as the sun.
I name this Dirk .....

*Consecration of the Dirk*

Bring it down in front of you, holding it with both hands at chest level. Concentrate all your power into the Dirk, seeing/sensing the power streaming from your

*Concentrate all your power into the Dirk*

Third Eye into it. Keep this up for several minutes, until you feel you have directed as much energy as you can.

For seven nights sleep with it under your pillow. From now on use the Dirk as much as you can; not only for ritual use but for mundane work also. The more you use it, the more it will absorb your mana.

*Consecration of the Keek-Stane*

## KEEK-STANE

The Keek-Stane must be consecrated at night, in the light of a Full Moon. It does not have to be done on a mountain top. (Though certainly it can be, if you prefer. In fact many of Aidan Breac's students plan all of their consecrations for the time of the full moon so that they can be on the Ben and do the Keek-Stane during the night then proceed to the morning sunrise for consecrating their Staff and Dirk.)

Sit or kneel on the ground with the Keek-Stane in front of you. Close your eyes and "feel" the energies of the Moon entering you and cleansing your body. Feel all the negativity being washed away as the white light fills you. Feel it traveling down your arms to your hands and down your legs to your feet. Breathe it in and absorb it.

Take up the Keek-Stane, with the lid of the box open, lying in the palms of your hands. Hold it up, as though offering it, to the Moon. Say:

> Smile down upon this Keek-Stane.
> Imbue it with love and honesty.
> Let it reflect, for me,
> Your wisdom and knowledge.
> Guard it from aught that is evil
> And let it ever have true sight.
> I name this Keek-Stane . . . . .

Draw the Keek-Stane down and breathe onto the glass. Do this three times, each time taking a deep breath. Feel that you are breathing life into the Stane. Then close your eyes and direct your energies into it; your power and strength.

The Keek-Stane should be set out (lid open) each full moon, for at least an hour every time, to replenish its energies. This should be in the open, or in an open window. Do not ever expose it to full sunlight. (It is possible to use it in a darkened room—or even a tent—during the daytime, if necessary, as will be explained later, but the best time to use it is during the hours between sunset and sunrise.)

## OTHER TOOLS

Any other tools (*e.g.* mool, quaich, censer, bell) do not have to be consecrated, though some people do give them a simple censing, in the smoke of incense, before they are first used. This, however, is not mandatory.

Similarly, the naming of the working tools, as described in the rituals above, is not mandatory. If you prefer not to name your Staff, Dirk, and/or Keek-Stane that is fine. Just leave that part out of the ritual(s).

# 6. The Solitary Witch

et us go back, for a moment, to the religiosity, or lack of it, in Pictish Witchcraft. In most other traditions of Wicca the participants get together regularly to worship and/or to work magick. There are celebrations of the Sabbats—four major and four minor—and Esbat workings at the New and Full Moons, oftimes with additional meetings on a weekly basis. The central core is a religious one, with worship as the backbone of the meetings. If there is a need to do magick, it is done at the Esbats. Most Solitary Wiccans also follow this pattern, worshipping alone and working their magick.

In most traditions of Wicca there is never a meeting where the Lord and the Lady are not called upon to attend and witness the rites. There is never a meeting—coven or solitary—where there are not prayers of thanks and occasional requests for help. Wicca is, as I have always pointed out in my books, lectures and workshops, a *religion*. It is recognized as such by both the federal government and the IRS.

But let me now draw a parallel with Christianity, for

example. Here, too, we find a variety of denominations, each practicing the religion assiduously, with regular meetings for worship; honoring their god and offering up prayers and requests for assistance. Yet here, too, we find any number of "solitary" Christians; those who seldom, if ever, attend formal services yet who staunchly declare themselves the most devout of their religion. They follow the tenets of Christianity, living their lives according to its teachings and believing-in/worshipping the deity, though not as formally as their church-going counterparts.

These latter we can compare to the PectiWita. PectiWitans are very decidedly believers in, and worshippers of, the Wiccan deities; the Lord and the Lady. In times of need they pray and ask for what they want. In times of joy they offer up their thanks. But, as with those "solitary" Christians, they do not feel the need for formalized rituals on a regular basis.

In the PectiWita there is not the backbone of religion. On occasions there may be reference to the gods, but these are far in the minority of occurences. Most Pictish Witches feel there is no need for a regular weekly, or monthly, religious practice. As with other Wiccans, he or she does "live" the path twenty-four hours a day, seven days a week . . . but as a practice, not necessarily as a religious path.

So what *does* the PectiWitan do? Very simply, you live as part of nature. You harmonize with nature and do not hesitate to use ("use" not "abuse") it to serve your ends. The use of herbs for healing the sick; the use of stones and roots for working magick; the use of all things that blend with your life and make your lot easier without harming others.

There are no separate occasions where a Witan would say, "*Now* I am practicing Witancraft," or "At this moment I am doing magick." Rather, *the Witan's whole life is part and parcel of Witancraft*. Eating a meal, sleeping, chopping wood, brewing herbs for a poultice, casting stones to divine the future, working a spell, herding sheep, or pruning a tree—these are all just part of life and, therefore, part of being a Witan.

## THE MAGICK SITE

Since magick plays a part—frequently a large part—in the Pictish Witch's life, let's look at that practice. Witan magick can be done almost anywhere. Yet, some places are necessarily better than others. The PectiWitan prefers height, so to be at some small area partway up or on the top of a mountain seems the ideal. Emphasizing the solitary aspect of the tradition, the need is certainly to be away from everyone and everything. He (or she, of course) needs to be somewhere where he can concentrate, where he will not be interrupted, where he is not overlooked. In the Highlands, away from even the most solitary cottage, is the ideal situation.

To relate this to the mundane world of American city living, you must think simply in terms of using a room with a locked door and with the telephone disconnected, and where there is no fear of interruption. But let me stay with the original, ideal, situation first. Then you can decide how that can be adapted to modern-day city living.

The size of the area is not too important. There is no nine-foot circle to be drawn; really no circle of any sort. If you can find a large, flat rock, or level tree stump, it would be a bonus but, again, that is not necessary. Most often there is no altar, or equivalent, used.

Frequently a small fire is lit beside your working area and, when burning well, natural fumigants are thrown on (*e.g.*, sweet flag, milfoil, catnip, etc.—see Chapter 4) to act like incense. Or, when ready, a piece of glowing wood can be taken from the fire and placed in the ritual area—on a piece of rock or in a depression in the ground—and sprinkled with the herbs or with actual incense.

That is all there is to the ritual site. There is no actual circle marked or ritually consecrated. No walking around with a sword, knife or staff, directing energy into the lines of a marked circle. No sprinkling salted water or censing with the incense.

What there is, to start with, is a "Centering." In effect this is a consecration; it is just not so in the generally accepted sense of Wiccan Circle-casting.

## CENTERING

Stand, facing east, with legs apart at about shoulder width. Hold your Staff before you with both hands at its top, the lower end of it on the ground to form a triangle with your two feet. Rest your head (forehead) on your hands, on the top of the Staff (this is a good reason for the Staff not to be too tall). With closed eyes, breathe deeply and feel the energies of the earth drawing up into your feet and legs. As you breathe, feel those earth energies gradually filling your body, driving out any negativity, tiredness, aches, pains, and the like. "See" the colors green and brown—the earth colors—flowing into you. Feel your feet firm upon the earth and know that you are centered and strong.

Continue this for as long as feels comfortable, then relax. You will quickly come to know when you are fully Centered.

*Centering*

## CIRCLE

F. Marian McNeill says (*The Silver Bough*):

> The Caledonians paid a superstitious reverence to the sun, and practically every religious festival began with the ceremony of walking thrice *deiseil*, that is, in a sunwise direction, round the circle, cairn, altar or bonfire that marked the site, the object of the rite being to aid the sun by virtue of mimetic magic.

This is certainly part of the teachings of Aidan Breac. *Deiseil* movement was considered lucky; *tuaithiuil*, or widdershins, or wrang-gaites, (counterclockwise) was unlucky. In ancient times, when warriors approached a fort they indicated whether they were friend or foe by advancing either *deiseil* or *tuaithiuil*. McNeill tells us that:

> Until recent times, expectant mothers went thrice round a church (*deiseil*) in order to ensure an easy delivery; fire was carried thrice round an infant before baptism to save it from the fate of a changeling; at a wedding, the company went thrice round the house before entering; sick persons thrice circulated a holy well before drinking the healing waters; boats putting out to sea thrice rowed about sunwise in order to ensure a safe passage or a good catch; even coffins were carried thus to the grave. The custom of going *deiseil* is far from having died out in the Highlands and the Islands.

After Centering, the Witan should walk three times, sunwise (*deiseil*), around in a circle. No special diameter; just what seems comfortable. My personal suggestion is to make it about six feet in diameter, around an imaginary center point—though, as I said above, there is no actual circle marked on the ground. Hold your Staff with both hands above your head, as you walk. It doesn't matter

*Walking the Circle*

where you start this circumnambulation, so long as it comprises three complete circuits. Then move to the east and plant the base of the Staff in the ground. Stand with legs slightly apart and gaze out to the east, holding the Staff with both hands.

A note here: anytime you stand with the Staff with its end on the ground in front of you, stand as in Centering so that your feet are about shoulder-distance apart and the Staff makes an equilateral triangle with your feet. Breac called this "the Basic Stance."

That is all there is to "Casting the Circle." No altar set-up; no deity figures; no salt, water and incense; no candles; no Sword or Wand. All very basic.

If at this point the Witan should feel inclined to talk with the gods, here is where he would summon/invite them. But, as stated, this is seldom done. More usually the Witan would now go straight into the working of necessary magick, meditation, the practice of divination, the making of talismans, the celebration of the season, "wind riding" (see below), or whatever was the reason for the ritual. In other words, all PectiWitan practices start with this Centering and Circle "Casting."

## WIND-RIDING

"To ride the wind" is an expression used by the Picts when talking of what is more generally known as astral projection. This is a practice much used by the PectiWita and effectively taught by Aidan Breac.

The body has an invisible double known variously as the "ethereal body" or "astral body." It is an exact duplicate of its physical counterpart though there are occasions when it may temporarily change its shape. This body can separate from the physical body when that is at rest—when you are asleep or in a trance state. By training yourself, through practice, you can separate at will and travel

*The Basic Stance*

wherever you wish. When your astral body returns, and you awake, you can have full remembrance of where your etheric double traveled. Many people do this traveling without realising it. What they remember of their astral journeys they think are simply dreams!

Aidan Breac's method of training is quite simple. It is based on the (light) trance method and can be done almost anywhere at any time.

Lie in the most comfortable position you can: on your back or side, it doesn't matter so long as you know you can lie that way for at least twenty minutes or so. You should be well rested, so there is no fear of you simply falling asleep. Many Pictish Witches do this in the early morning, when they have already had a good night's sleep.

You need to attain that hazy borderline between being awake and being asleep. With your eyes closed, breathe deeply and gradually relax your whole body. A good way to do this is to go through a "checklist": start with your feet and concentrate on relaxing them. Then feel that relaxation move up to your ankles and lower legs. Concentrate and make them relax. Feel all the muscles relaxing; all the tension and tiredness flowing out of them. Move that on up to the upper legs and feel them relax. Work next on the lower torso. Feel the stomach muscles relaxing. Feel your lower back relaxing. Make it happen that you sink down into a wonderful, comfortable sense of ease.

Continue through with the rest of your body: upper torso, fingers, hands, arms, shoulders, neck, head. Get every single part of you to totally relax and feel at ease.

When all the body has been covered in this way, and you are completely at ease, then—with your eyes still closed—start to think of your surroundings. The spot where you lay; the nearby rocks and trees; the slope down to the burn; the trees on the far side. If you are indoors, think of the settee where you lay; the coffee table; chairs; pictures on the walls. See everything around you, even though your eyes are closed.

The first few times you do this you may not be able to fill in everything. Don't worry; keep practicing. Suddenly you will realise that you are not just imagining . . . you are actually looking at these things!

At this stage, or even slightly before, you may feel a strange sensation: a numbness that starts at your feet and gradually moves up through your whole body. This sensation is actually the separation of your astral body from your physical body. You will find you have absolutely no wish whatsoever to move. You will be content to lie still. You may think to yourself that, if you really wanted to, you could move an arm, or a leg . . . but you just can't be bothered! All that is necessary now is to will your astral body to separate completely; to move up and out of your physical body. You will find that indeed you do move out. You will be able to stand up alongside your sleeping physical body.

It sometimes happens that, as you lie there relaxed and breathing deeply, you will get a sudden feeling that your eyes are rolling upwards. It is almost as though you are looking up and backwards into your own brain; towards the pineal gland. You may then get a sensation of rushing upwards, towards the top of your head, until you suddenly find yourself standing, calmly and in peace, beside your own self. This is known as Exiting by the Pineal Door. Occasionally this is accompanied by what seems like a shaking and shuddering. It doesn't often happen but don't be afraid if it does.

Should you ever be in a state of partial release—half in your body and half out—don't worry. You may lift your astral arms but feel the rest of you is tied down! Just relax and tell yourself that if your upper body is ready there's no reason why the rest shouldn't be. You should slip out quite easily then.

Very probably when you first leave your body you will experience dual consciousness. You will feel yourself in your astral body, standing up, but at the same time you will feel yourself in your physical body, lying down. Just concentrate on the "you" in the astral body and go on your way.

How to go on your way? Breac says to listen to the wind. All your senses are more finely attuned in the astral state. No matter how gentle the breeze, you will be aware of it. Now, says Breac, ride with it! Step up and off the ground and feel yourself carried by the wind, "riding" it. It will take you wherever you want to go. Whenever you are ready to return, it will bring you back.

You can actually journey with the speed of thought, in the astral state. Just think of where you want to be and you will be there. Similarly, you can return to your body in no time at all.

There is often talk of the so-called "dangers" of astral projection. When your astral body moves off it is connected to your physical body by an infinitely elastic silver-colored cord. Usually this goes from navel to navel, like a long umbilical cord. In popular fantasy/fiction it is said that if this cord is severed you cannot get back to your body! Don't worry about it; there is virtually no way it can get severed. And don't forget, you can be back in your body in the speed of thought. We have no evidence of anyone ever having died because their "silver cord" was accidentally cut, so don't worry about it.

PectiWitans use Wind Riding to visit other places, far away. Sometimes they need to know what is happening at a distance. Rather than using the Keek Stane, many will Wind Ride. The more you do it, the more practiced you become at it, the easier it becomes.

# 7. Magickal Power Raising

here are many different ways of working magick; of making things happen. After all, that's all magick is . . . making something happen that you want to happen. In this book I will be dealing with the ways used by the PectiWita. I say "that's all it is," but don't be misled. Magick is not done on a whim (or shouldn't be!). It is done only when there is a very real need. It is done when it seems that what you want cannot be achieved any other way. Most methods involve some form of "power raising"; of amassing sufficient energy to send out and cause change to occur. This takes effort. It can be a lot of work. So, you see, magick is not an easy short-cut to achieving something because you can't be bothered to get it any other way. Magick is, or should be, in effect, a last resort. It should be something you do after you have tried everything else you can think of.

## MAGICKAL ETHICS

There is one law found throughout Witchcraft. It applies equally to the PectiWita and to all other forms of Wicca. Aidan Breac used to beat it into the heads of his students and so do I. That law is "AN IT HARM NONE, DO WHAT THOU WILT." The old word "an" means "if." So it is saying, if it harms no one, you can do what you like. But there is that modifier there—*if* it harms no one, and *only* if it harms no one, you can do anything you like. So always carefully think through what you are planning to do. Will it *in any way* harm anyone (and this includes yourself, of course)? If it will—or if it will in any way interfere with someone else's free will—then YOU MUST NOT DO IT! And that's all there is to be said.

So always, as the very first thing you must do when planning magick, sit down and think through, very carefully, the repercussions of your intended action. Who might it affect and how?

I sometimes hear it said that you cannot/should not do magick for yourself. This is totally incorrect. Not only *can* you do magick for yourself, but you are the *best* person to do magick for you. By that I mean, the person most qualified to work magick is the person the magick will most directly affect. If you need a job, *you* are the one most in need, most immediately affected. Thereby *you* are the one most able to put energy into the working. Someone else working for you is not going to have that same emotional involvement and therefore not going to raise as much power. So, far from not working magick for yourself, you should *always* work magick for yourself!

To take that a step further, if someone else asks you to work magick for them, say no. If at all possible try to get them to do the work themselves. (It's not always possible but many times it is.) Show them how, by all means. Even, if necessary, work *with* them. But get them to do the major portion of the work. The results will be far more positive.

Historically, certainly, Witches were the ones who

worked their magick for others. But that was for several reasons, among them the fact that in the past most others were too ignorant and too unwilling to learn. Today, if someone is interested enough, and knowledgeable enough to believe that magick can be done, then they are usually intelligent enough to take instruction in how to do it.

## PREPARATION FOR MAGICK

Think carefully through what you want to achieve in your magickal working. Decide, especially, on the end product. For example: suppose you want to get a new job (or a better job, or a promotion). Think about that job—exactly what type of position do you want? How much responsibility can you handle? What salary would be fair? What sort of hours can you work? In other words, don't just think in general terms of "getting a job." Think in specifics. This way, when working the magick you will have a clear-cut picture of the end product—of exactly what you are trying to achieve. In magick, focus is one of the most important ingredients.

Having decided exactly what you are asking for (and always keep in mind the old adage: "Be careful of what you ask for . . . you just may get it!"), now decide on the method you are going to use to obtain it. A lot of, though by no means all, magick done by PectiWitans is of the sympathetic, or imitative, variety, based on the law that "like attracts like." Whichever method you use, however, there will be a need to raise "power" (for want of a better word). But before we look at power raising, we need to examine Visualization.

## VISUALIZATION

*The secret of visualizing is to know: More important than seeing with your eyes is seeing with your heart.*

—Lazarus

I've said that focus is one of the most important ingredients of magick; to be able to focus exactly on what it is you want. As outlined above, you should have a perfectly clear idea of what this is, and all the ramifications of what you are setting out to achieve. Having got that, you now need to be able to visualize that desire. Some people claim they cannot visualize anything. I once met a man who said he couldn't even close his eyes and see the face of his mother, or his wife, let alone visualize something like the result of a magickal act! Few people are as bad as that.

To learn to visualize, start small. Sit comfortably in a chair and look at an object on a table in front of you. It can be something as mundane as an apple or a book. If you are outdoors, focus on a leaf or a rock. Concentrate on that object and see all its component parts. Let's take the example of a book; see the cover and the binding, see their color and fabric (cloth, leather, paper). See the illustration, title, author on the cover or dustjacket, if there is one. Even look hard at the edges of the pages that are visible. See if they are neatly trimmed or ragged. See everything about the book. Then close your eyes and continue to see it. "Examine" it, with your eyes closed. If you get really stuck, simply open your eyes again for a moment and review what is there. Then close them again.

Do this with a variety of objects, getting more and more complex. When you have no trouble keeping images in your mind's eye, then go on to "seeing" objects that you have not just been studying but that you are fairly familiar with . . . the family car, for example. See its color, shape and form, details of the doors, windshield, etc.

The Haitian bocor, Boko Gédé, teaches visualization by having his students study a photograph of a particular scene. He will then tear the photograph in half and lay one half on a sheet of white paper. The student can then "fill in" the missing half from his mind. With permission, I detailed this method in my book *Buckland's Complete Book of Witchcraft*.

The final step is to visualize something you have not actually seen before, such as a scene from history, for practice . . . Washington crossing the Delaware, for example. When you can do that—when you can visualize a whole scene and be able to focus in on any detail within it—then you are ready to work your magick.

## POWER RAISING

I have discussed the inner power we all possess in most of my previous books on Witchcraft. It is something which everyone has within them, but which some can bring out more strongly than others. The Polynesian word *mana* is sometimes used for this power. Aidan Breac used the Scottish word *maucht* (pronounced "maw-kt," or "maw-cht" with a guttural "ch"), meaning energy, or power. Your *maucht* is what is responsible for those flashes of ESP you sometimes experience; for causing someone in a crowd to turn and look at you when you want them to; for creating a situation that you desperately desire to be there. The power given off by sacred objects and holy sites, can also be described as *maucht*. *Maucht* is the power underlying all forms of magick. It is the means by which sickness can be cured . . . or caused. It is like electricity, for example, in that it is simply a "power," and the operator can decide whether to use that power for good or for evil.

How can you generate that power? The secret seems

to be in working yourself up into *ekstasis*, or "ecstasy"; in "getting out of yourself." This is so in virtually all forms of magick found around the world, not just in Pictish magick. In Gardnerian, and similar forms of Wicca, this *ekstasis* is induced by dancing. Starting slowly and then gradually working up to fever pitch causes the blood to course through the body and, in turn, generates the power needed to perform the magick.

In the PectiWita dancing can also be done, though it is not essential. If you are to dance, then there is no set form to it; no choreographed set of steps. It is free-form. It is more of a movement with a regular, rhythmic beat.

To practice, find a recording of a good, steady, rhythmic drum beat. There are many good Haitian drum recordings, Amerindian rhythms, African drums, and the like (see *Bibliography*). Or you can stick with the Scottish theme and go with the beat of some rousing Highland reel. I'd suggest avoiding the strathspeys (too slow) and the jigs (too "jumpy"). The main thing is, to get the "feel" of moving to a strong, hard beat; to be able to move around within a small area, in a freeform style of dance/movement. Listen for the emphases to the rhythms. Bang your feet onto the ground in time with those strong beats. Then practice doing it without the recorded music.

With practice—and some will need more than others—you will be able to really work yourself up into a sweat, swinging around to the beat that is in your head. And this is the start of "getting out of yourself." In Chapter Eleven I give more details of actual dance steps you might try.

To achieve this same pitch of excitement without actually dancing can be done. Try it sitting in a chair, or on the ground. Listen to that same exciting music and let your body just sort of move/rock with the beat. By rocking and moving your arms and tapping your feet, clapping your hands, it is possible to work up to much the same state of *ekstasis* as is done by actually dancing around.

So now that you know how to decide on what you want, to focus on it, and to work yourself up into the necessary pitch of excitement to generate the power needed to achieve it, what then? The actual releasing of that power and directing it to achieve your end—the final step in the working of magick—I will detail in the next chapter. But first, I would like to touch on "grounding." Grounding is getting rid of excess *maucht*. Sometimes, when releasing the power, not all of it goes. This should not be a problem, since it is positive energy that has been generated. However, some few people do find themselves affected to the point of staying hyped unless they ground the excess energy.

## GROUNDING

This is good to do after magick, whether or not you feel it necessary to ground. Stand, barefoot and legs apart, and close your eyes. Take a number of good, deep breaths and calm your body. Feel energy—the life force—pulsating around your body. Feel/sense your body filled with the white light of *maucht*. Now direct that energy down, through the soles of your feet, into the ground beneath you. If you have to be in a building just do the same thing, directing it down into the floorboards, and sense the energy going on down, through the building, until it reaches the earth below. If you wish to sit to do this, simply place your hands, palm down, on the ground beside you and follow the same procedure.

Breac suggested that it might be helpful to imagine a thermometer, with red liquid high up in it. As you calm yourself, see the level of the liquid falling; see it dropping down as you gradually drop down in energy level. With this visualization, you can stop and retain any energy level that feels good, or you can let it all seep away to nothing. Continue until you feel completely calmed and relaxed. Then you may open your eyes.

Next chapter I will tell you how to encompass these techniques in the actual working of magick.

# 8. Working Magick —"the Airts"

he art of magick has always been a practical affair for the PectiWita. It had to bring rain, increase the flocks and herds, cure sickness, strengthen bonds of love, or protect from the evil eye. Its performance was a learned art, or *airt*, which took time to learn. The Pictish Witches took that time; they trained long and hard. Consequently they were much sought after by the common people ("common" in the sense of being unlearned in "the airts").

## THE POWER OF THOUGHT

"Thoughts are things" goes the old saying. This is certainly true from the magickal perspective. By putting power—*maucht*—into your thoughts, and directing that, you are able to manifest whatever you wish. By working out all the details of that which you wish to create, then achieving *ekstasis* to help generate the *maucht*, you can direct the power to cause change to occur. As Aleister Crowley so aptly put it: "[magick is] causing change to occur in conformity with will" ... making happen what you want to happen.

You now have all the ingredients for working magick. Let's put them together. At the end of Chapter 6 you were left standing facing east after having Centered and then walked three times deiseil. Let's presume you now wish to go on to work magick.

While standing in the Basic Stance, gather your thoughts together to go over, one final time, the steps you are going to take (you should have done all your planning ahead of starting the actual ritual, of course). Know what the end result is to be and come to focus on that. Concentrate. *See* that final result. Let's again take the example of getting a job. See yourself working at the job. See yourself in the surroundings in which you will be working. See yourself doing all the things the job would entail. You are there! You *have* the job! Know that.

If you prefer, rather than remaining in the Basic Stance for this final review, you can adopt "the crouch." This is the position you took up briefly when consecrating the Staff. It is often used by Pictish Witches in everyday life for a brief rest. You simply sit astride your Staff, with it at an angle, taking the weight on the upper part of the Staff with your arms across your knees.

. When you have completed this final review, now start dancing. You can either dance with your Staff (many Witans do) or you can lay it down and dance without it. (If you don't want to dance to generate the maucht, I'll treat that approach in a moment.)

Remember the strong, steady, throbbing beat; the rhythmic movement you have practiced. Work at it. Hear the music, the sound, in your head. Close your eyes and go with it. Let yourself get worked up, get carried away. Dance around and around, getting more and more into the feel of it. And, as you dance, bring your thoughts back to that job. As you dance, see yourself there, working. *See* yourself. *Know* that you have that job! Dance, turn, spin—just direct all your energies into that solid thought of having the job. Keep this up for just as long as you can . . . then a little while longer! When you can do no more, stop—collapse onto the ground if necessary—and release the thought. Let it go, and just calm yourself. Slowly bring yourself back, taking deep breaths and grounding yourself if you have to.

Some Witans like to release the power with a shout, and I think that is a good idea. Choose a word appropriate to the aim of the magickal work. In the above example you were working to get a job, so the very word "job" would do. It doesn't have to be any mystical, esoteric word . . . just something basic and appropriate. The shorter the word the better. In other words a one-syllable word would be preferable to a three-syllable one—"job" would be better than "employment." It is merely a verbal focus for you when releasing the power. So, when you reach that high point, where you have built up the power just as much as you possibly can, then drop to the ground and shout. Let the power go with the word.

In Chapter Ten I tell you how you can charge your Staff with power. If you have done this, then you can here release that power also, to supplement what you have now raised. In this case, dance with the Staff. When you reach the release stage you not only shout your word, but you raise and *shake* the Staff, releasing that power also.

In Chapter Eleven—"Song and Dance"—I talk about another tool that can be used. This is the *Sùil Dhè mhóir* ("The Eye of the Great God"). As I describe in that chapter, it is marked on the ground and the dance starts out all around the symbol, gradually moving in on it and, finally, dancing over it and stamping it into the ground.

If you don't want to dance, you can still work yourself up as I described in the previous chapter. Lay down your Staff in front of you and sit. Then work by rocking, shaking, beating your hands on the ground, on your thighs, on your body—whatever it takes. Follow the same pattern as above, hearing the rhythm in your head, working up to ecstacy and then releasing the energy into the thought of having the job. Keep it up for as long as you can, then release with a shout and come down. Ground yourself. If you're using the charged Staff, grab it up at the release point and shake it as you shout.

This is one way—a very effective, time-tested way—of working magick. But, of course, it is not the only way. Far from it.

## IMITATIVE MAGICK

Some people need to be able to actually see what they are working on, in order to concentrate their energies. For them many forms of sympathetic magick are easier. Most people are familiar with the idea of what is frequently (incorrectly) termed a "voodoo doll"—a cloth or wax figure that has, for example, pins stuck into it. This is an excellent example of this type of magick. The doll has been made to represent someone in particular. By the Black Magician ("Black" in the sense of a worker of negative magick) directing his or her energies into that figure through the agency of the pins, he/she is in effect putting that negativity into the very person the figure represents. On the positive side, a White Magician (worker of positive magick) can effect a cure on someone who is sick by filling a cloth doll (representing the patient) with healing herbs.

Remembering that PectiWitans do not do negative magick—"An it harm none..."—then imitative magick is a very effective way of working and one which they frequently use.

"Like attracts like" is the rule. Take something to represent someone. If you are working on yourself then you can make an image of yourself, in cloth, wax, clay, wood, or whatever. Consecrating that figure (see below), you can then do to it anything you would like to bring upon yourself. You can use other objects in conjunction with that figure. For example, in many Gypsy charms and spells acorns are used to symbolize strength (see my book *Secrets of Gypsy Love Magick*, Llewellyn 1990). By filling with acorns a cloth "poppet" of yourself you would, symbolically, be imbuing yourself with strength.

If you have a broken leg, you could make a wax figure to represent yourself, break the leg off it and then, in ritual, gently warm the wax and blend the leg back together again. In that way you would, symbolically, be

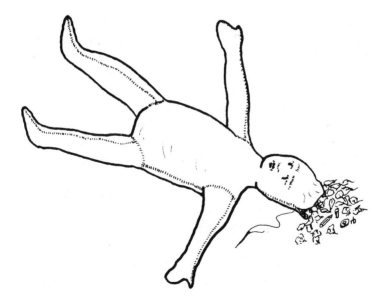

*An acorn-filled poppet.*

mending your broken leg; or at the very least helping it to heal. Note: have the leg broken off the figure *before* you actually name/consecrate the figure to represent you! In other words (i) make the figure, thinking of yourself; (ii) *clear your thoughts* and break off the leg; (iii) re-attach the leg just by sticking the two ends together; (iv) again thinking of yourself, consecrate the figure, naming it for yourself; (v) do the magick of working on the join to blend the two parts of the leg together again as one whole section. As you blend the two parts together again, see yourself (or whomever, if you are doing it for someone else) running about, jumping, hopping, skipping, etc. See them actually using the leg, with it being completely well again.

In these, and similar, examples there is no need for the figure to look exactly like the person it is intended to represent. It can be quite a crude representation. But in making it, you must have a clear picture of that person in mind. Having a photograph handy, which you can keep looking at while you are making the figure, is a big help.

To make the figure even more personal you might include actual items from the individual, such as nail parings, hair, cloth from their clothing, or similar. You should mark the figure with the person's name, and could also add such additional personalizations as their astrological signs (sun, moon, rising). The figures can be just as elaborate or just as simple as you care to make them. But they do need this personalization; this tying-in with the very person they represent.

In the Highlands of Scotland wax was not easy to come by, so many of the Pecti-Witches of old would use clay. Their images were called *corp creadha*, which actually means "clay body" or "clay corpse." John Gregorson Campbell, in his *Witchcraft and Second Sight In the Highlands and Islands of Scotland* (1902), tells the story of MacIain Ghiarr, which illustrates the use of such a figure:

MacIain Ghiarr, the Ardnamurchan thief, stole so many cattle from MacLean of Dowart that he made that chief his deadly enemy. On one of his roving expeditions (MacIain) was passing at midnight the chapel or burying ground of Pennygown (*caibel Peighinn-a-ghobhan*), on the Sound of Mull. Seeing a light in the chapel, he entered, and found three witches sticking pins in a *corp creadha* intended to represent MacLean of Dowart. As each pin was stuck in, MacLean was seized with a stitch in the corresponding part of his body. Only the last pin remained to be stuck in. It was to be in the heart, and to cause death. MacIain Ghiarr scattered the witches, took with him the clay corpse, and made his way to MacLean, whom he found at death's door. He took out in his presence the pins one by one, and when the last pin was taken out MacLean jumped up a hale man, and remained ever after the warm friend of MacIain Ghiarr.

Why the Witches were working negative magick, we are not told. Negative magick was not uncommon in the old days. However, today we stress—Work no ill. An it harm none, do what thou wilt.

## CONSECRATION

I have spoken of consecrating the figure. This is just a personalization, similar to a Christian baptism. You take the figure, once it has been completely made, and hold it in the smoke of incense—Wolf Claw and Common Nettle, or sandalwood, would be good. Turning it in the smoke, so that all parts are censed, say something to this effect:

"I here present myself (or the name of the person you are working for). This poppet *is* me (or name, again) in every way, so that anything I do to this poppet I do to myself (or name)."

Hold it up to the sun (or moon, if working at night)

for a few moments then in the smoke of the incense again. Say "So may it be!"

You can use your own words for this, if you'd rather, so long as the sense is of naming the poppet.

## COMBINED FORMS

You could combine the above two methods: visualization and imitative. Suppose you dearly want/need a new car. You should know the type, make, model, price of the one you want. Make a model of it. As with the human figure, it doesn't have to be geometrically exact, but do have a clear picture in your head or a photograph of it beside you as you work. In fact, why not move with the times? These days it is possible to find a plastic assembly model kit of many cars. Buy one of those and put it together, concentrating on seeing it as *your* car. Paint it the color you want. Then, using that as a focal point for your concentration before starting building up the *maucht*, see yourself in that car. See yourself driving it. See it in your garage. Some people find such an artifact a useful tool in getting them started on their visualization.

There are probably hundreds, if not thousands, of variations on sympathetic, or imitative, magick. Let your imagination run rampant. As I have said, this is one of the most popular forms of magick among the Pictish Witches.

## PICTISH RITUALS

Pictish Witches do not go in for much in the way of formalized rituals. Rather than passing out copies of approved rituals, Aidan Breac would work with his students on what amounted to extemporization: how to come up with an appropriate form of magick to suit the particular occasion. However, we might say that there are five main headings for magick to be worked. These are: HEALTH, WEALTH, LOVE, PROTECTION, POWER.

Any problem you come up against, for which you wish to work magick, can be placed under one or other of these five headings. You therefore really only need to think in terms of five basic rituals, which can be modified for individual cases.

**Health** is usually dealt with by the use of poppets (wax or clay poppets, or cloth poppets filled with healing herbs), or by visualization. Non-magickally, of course, by treatment with medicinal herbs.

With **Wealth** it is worth mentioning that magick does not seem to work when you are trying to acquire wealth simply for the sake of having it. If there is a very real need for you to have money—to pay a pressing bill, meet your mortgage payment, obtain transportation, or similar— then you can get what you need (but seldom more!). This is probably why there are few rich Witches!

**Love** can be treated in many ways. Poppets are popular, but here you must beware of making a poppet of a *specific individual* and interfering with his or her free will. Remember, that would be classed as black magick. Work on yourself, to make yourself so attractive that you *naturally* draw the one you desire. Or make a poppet of the *type* of person you desire: dark haired, tall, attractive, etc. There are a multitude of ethical ways of working love magick sympathetically. Put your imagination to work.

**Protection**, again, lends itself to imitative magick. (For example, make a poppet of yourself and then wrap it in an oak leaf, representing strength and protection.) For the removal of problems, be they curses, sicknesses, bad luck, or whatever, remember to work in the dark of the moon. That is, from after the full moon through to the new moon. All other work should be done in the waxing moon: from the new moon through to the full.

I cannot think of many **Power** rituals that could not be classified under one or other of the other four headings. As with wealth, you cannot get power for power's sake. You cannot get power to wield over others—again, you would be interfering with their freewill. But you might want power for yourself to overcome some bad habit (though this might better be looked at under the health heading). Or power to move up in your employment (though this might come down to a desire to make more money, and therefore fall under wealth rather than power). Always think very carefully when you are drawn towards the word "power." Don't forget, always, to consider the ramifications of what you are setting out to achieve... will this affect anyone else in any way? Especially, will this harm anyone?

One thing you might want to have ready for these different types of ritual is the incense. It can help to use a special incense to create the right vibrations for a particular purpose. I mentioned some few basic incenses in Chapter Four. For magick many PectiWitans will use one or more of the following:

For HEALTH—Allspice, calamus, pine, cedar, fennel, mugwort, myrrh, oak, rosemary, sandalwood, thyme, willow.

For WEALTH—Basil, chamomile, cinquefoil, clover, dill, elder, jasmine, myrtle, nutmeg, oak, staghorn, vervain, woodruff.

For LOVE— Apple, basil, catnip, chamomile, chickweed, dill, geranium, jasmine, lavender, lemon verbena, rose, Scotch heather, sweet flag, thyme, vervain, yarrow.

For PROTECTION—Basil, frankincense, horehound, juniper, lilac, mistletoe, myrrh, pine, sandalwood, thistle.

For POWER—Allspice, basil, cedar, clover, fennel, jasmine, oak, pine, staghorn, yarrow.

## HISTORIC SCOTTISH MAGICK

Scottish history and legend is replete with stories of magickal workings, spells and charms. A lot of this reflects the very forms of the *airt* used by the PectiWita. A few examples follow.

In Orkney there is a charm performed to bring a good supply of butter. The Witan will go to the seashore with a pail or bowl. From the first large incoming wave that she sees she will count nine more waves. At the reflux of this ninth one she will quickly scoop up three *gowpens* of the water and drop them into the pail. (A *gowpen* is as much as can be held in the two cupped hands.) The water is carried home and put into the churn with the milk. It is said to always produce a good supply of butter.

To ensure a favorable breeze, fishermen and seamen at Gourock Bay by Kempoch Point in the southwest of Scotland would pace seven times *deiseil* around a large monolith standing on the cliffs. As they walked around they sang a plea for fair winds. The monolith has since become known as "Granny Gourock," some say in rememberance of an old Witan woman who could whistle up the wind.

In Moray, the Pechts would cut down withes of woodbine in the waxing of the March moon. These they would twist into wreaths and preserve for a year and a day. After that time young children suffering from fever and consumption would be passed three times through the wreaths and thus be cured.

Even today throughout the Highlands many people carry a "lucky penny," known in Gaelic as *peighinn pisich*. This has to be turned over three times, in the pocket, at the first glimpse of the new moon.

Of well and water magick, there are examples such as the well at Willie's Muir, in Aberdeenshire. Barren women would go to where the water came out between several stones. There they would take off their shoes and stockings, roll up their skirts and, naked to the waist, dance around (deiseil) in the water, splashing their genitals.

Water was sometimes drunk at healing wells from the horn of a living cow. McNeill suggests that the belief could have been that life from the animal might be thus communicated. The power of foretelling life or death was supposedly conferred on the Dripping Well at Avoch, Ross-shire, by the Brahan Seer. If you went to drink the water from the well, for healing purposes, you should first float two straws in the water. If they whirl around in opposite directions it means you will recover; if they lie motionless, you will soon die.

In some parts of Aberdeenshire it was believed that if you take half of the root of the orchis and get someone of the opposite sex to eat it, it will cause them to have a strong attraction to you. The other half of the root would cause a strong repulsion. Often, when the roots of the orchis are dug up, the old root is found to be dried up and the new root fresh and full. If the old root is taken, dried, and ground up, it is supposed to work as a wonderful love potion.

There is an endless variety of superstitions regarding actions which are unlucky. For example, it is unlucky for a stranger to count your sheep, cattle or children. If someone asks "How many children have you?" it is common to add "Bless them" to the reply. It is unlucky if a stranger steps across a parcel of fishing-poles on the beach, or over ropes, oars, or sailing gear when a boat is about to put out to sea. Means are used to get the stranger to retrace his steps.

It is unlucky to drink the health of company, or to serve them drinks or food around a table except it be done deiseil. It is unlucky to set off anywhere—in a boat, a marriage or funeral procession, even walking—unless it is to the right (deiseil).

It is unlucky to hear the cuckoo, or see a foal or snail before breakfast. In fact there is an old Gaelic rhyme to this effect:

> *Chunnaic mi an searrachan 'sa chulaobh rium,*
> *Chunnaic mi an t-seilcheag air an lic luim;*
> *Chual mi' a' chuag gun ghreim 'nam bhroinn,*
> *Is dh' aithnich mi fein nach rachadh a' bhliadhn' so*
> *leam.*

This roughly translates as:

> With its back to me turn'd I beheld the young foal,
> And the snail on the bare flag in motion so slow;
> Without taste of food, lo! the cuckoo I heard,
> Then judged that the year would not prosperously
> go.

In Shetland there was once a belief that it was unlucky to save a drowning man! It is still unlucky to throw out water after sunset and before sunrise. It is unlucky to have a grave open on a Sunday, for another will be dug within the week, it is said, for another member of that family. And if a corpse does not stiffen after death, there will be another death in the family before the end of the year.

The howling of a dog at night and the resting of a crow or magpie on the housetop are warnings of death. Cats sleeping near infants suck their breath and kill them. When children begin to walk they must go upstairs before they go downstairs, otherwise they will not thrive in the world. If there is no stair they must climb a chair.

If you rock an empty cradle you will soon be rocking a new baby in it. With this superstition, it is amusing to see the look of alarm that passes across the face of a woman who has a large family when one of her children happens to rock an empty cradle! She will rush across the room to stop it.

It is unlucky to catch sight of the new moon through a window. It is a token of fine weather to see the new moon with its "horns" turned up, since they retain the water that would fall to earth if they were turned down. If when fishing you count what you have taken, you will take no more.

There are literally hundreds, if not thousands, of such charms and superstitions and John Gregorson Campbell's *Witchcraft and Second Sight in the Highlands and Islands of Scotland* is replete with them.

# 9. Seership

oinneach Odhar Fiosaiche, Kenneth Mackenzie (or Kenneth the Sallow), is usually referred to as "The Brahan Seer." He is as famous in Scotland as Nostrodamus is elsewhere. Kenneth was born at Baile-na-Cille, in the parish of Uig, on the island of Lewis, around the beginning of the seventeenth century. Nothing much is recorded about his early life. He grew up to work as a laborer on the Brahan Estate, hence his appellation. He is regarded as beyond comparison the most distinguished of all the Highland Seers.

The gift of prophesy, "second sight," or *an da shealladh*, is an ages old belief in the Highlands. The Brahan Seer's prophesies were recited from generation to generation, for many years before they were fulfilled; some of them have been fulfilled in our own day; some few still remain to be fulfilled.

According to legend, when in his early teens Kenneth Mackenzie had a ready wit and a sharp tongue. The wife of the farmer he worked for didn't take kindly to either his practical jokes nor to his mockery of her assumed airs. Apparently she came to so dislike him that she planned to poison him! One day Kenneth had been out cutting peats, or divots, to be used for fuel, and was very tired. Waiting for the farmer's wife to bring his lunch out to the fields to him, he lay down to rest. Unknown to him, he was lying on the side of a fairy hill, and there he fell asleep.

Kenneth suddenly awoke to discover a small, white stone, with a hole through the middle of it, lying on his chest. He picked it up. As he came awake and examined the stone, he held it up and squinted through it. Through the hole he saw the farmer's wife coming across the fields, bringing his lunch. But, to his surprise, the stone gave him the ability to "see" that the lunch she carried was poisoned. When he received it, and after the woman was gone, he fed it to a collie. The dog writhed and died in agony.

One account says that Kenneth lost the sight in the eye he first used to gaze through the stone, and became *cam*, or blind in one eye. Whether or not he then continued to gaze with that (blind) eye, or whether he risked the good one is not recorded, but ever after he could look through the hole in the stone and see into the future.

There are a number of famous prophesies that Kenneth made. One was that "the time will come, and it is not far off, when full-rigged ships will be seen sailing eastward and westward by the back of Tomnahurich, near Inverness." About a hundred years later the Caledonian Canal was built around the back of Tomnahurich Hill. Another startling prophesy was "that the day will come when Tomnahurich,"—or, as he called it, Tom-na-sithichean, or the Fairy Hill, "will be under lock and key, and the fairies secured within." The *Inverness Advertiser*, in 1859, ran a paragraph:

Tomnahurich, the far-famed Fairies' Hill, has been sown with oats. According to tradition, the Brahan prophet, who lived 200 years ago, predicted that ships with unfurled sails would pass and repass Tomnahurich; and further, that it would yet be placed under lock and key. The first part of the prediction was verified with the opening of the Caledonian Canal, and we seem to be on the eve of seeing the realization of the rest by the final closing up of the Fairies' Hill.

Indeed, a short time later a cemetery occupied the top of the hill, with the spirits (of the dead) securely chained within.

Although there were virtually no established roads in the Highlands, Kenneth said that "the day will come when there will be a road through the hills of Ross-shire from sea to sea, and a bridge upon every stream." He prophesied the battle of Culloden. At Culloden itself he said:

This bleak moor, ere many generations have passed, shall be stained with the best blood of Scotland. Glad am I that I shall not see the day.

Many were the predictions Kenneth made about Scottish families—"The day will come when the Mackenzies will lose all their possessions in Lochlash..." "We shall have a fair-haired Lochiel; a red-haired Lovat; a squint-eyed, fair-haired Chisholm; a big, deaf Mackenzie..." "...the old wife with the footless stocking will drive the Lady of Clan Ranald from Nunton House..." All of these, and more, came to pass. The greatest of them, however, was the foretelling of the doom of the great House of Seaforth. The Countess of Seaforth had repeatedly demanded to know, from Kenneth, what her lord was doing on his trip to Paris. The Seer tried to be evasive but finally told her all he saw—the third Earl of Seaforth was living it up with the ladies of the French court! In her rage at hearing this, the Countess had Kenneth taken away and burned to death in a tar-barrel, as a Witch. But before he died he predicted the doom of Seaforth in great detail. It came to be fulfilled in extraordinary minuteness.

Thomas the Rhymer—Thomas Rimor de Ercildun—was another, earlier, great Scottish seer. He was from the thirteenth century, lived in the west of Berwickshire, and prophesied the Battle of Bannockburn, the union of the Scottish and English crowns, the Battle of Pinkie (1547), the banishment of the last Earl Marischal (1746) and the forfeiture of Marischal's lands of Inverugie, among many other things.

## SECOND SIGHT

As I said earlier, second sight is an ages old belief in the Highlands. And it is a practice that was taught by Aidan Breac. The Gaelic *da-shealladh* does not literally mean "second sight" but, rather, "the two sights". The object "seen" is often called *taibhs* (pronounced "tay-ish"), the person seeing it *taibhsear* (pr. "tay-isher"), and the gift of vision, in addition to being called "second sight", called *taibhsearachd*.

According to John Campbell:

> The shepherds of the Hebrid Isles are usually cred-
> ited with the largest possession of the gift, but the
> doctrine was well-known over the whole Highlands,
> and as firmly believed in Ross-shire and the high-
> lands of Perthshire as in the remotest Hebrides.

The Picts were believed to possess second sight to a high degree. It is not surprising, therefore, that one of the working tools of the PectiWita is the Keek Stane, or "Seeing Stone," and that divination should be one of their major practices.

The *frith* was a spell used in the Highlands to discover the condition of someone at a distance, especially a person or animal that was lost. It was done on the first Monday of the Quarter, before sunrise. The *Frithear* would be barefoot and bareheaded and would have fasted. He, or she, would walk deiseil around the house, with eyes closed, till the doorstep was reached. There he would open his eyes and look out through a circle made by his finger and thumb. He then judged by the character of the omen he saw as he first looked through. The possible sights were numerous, of course. If it was something that could be judged as a sacred symbol—such as two straws or pieces of wood crossed, symbolizing the sun—then all was well. A man standing was a positive sign, meaning health or recovery; a woman standing was a negative sign. A red-haired woman was unlucky; black-haired, lucky.

## USING THE KEEK STANE

The Keek Stane is never used in direct sunlight. It can be used in shade, if necessary, but by far the best results are obtained if it is used after the sun has set and/or before it has risen. Breac said that the very best results of all were obtained in the light of the full moon.

Incense can be scattered on the fire as an aid. Again, a natural burning herb is recommended, such as Breac's favorite: sweet flag (*Acorus calamus*), or juniper (*Juniperus communis*), sandalwood, or myrrh. One tip—don't sit where the smoke is blowing over you. It may seem pleasant for a while but it will quickly detract from what you are trying to achieve. Sit upwind of the fire, so that you can concentrate on the Keek Stane.

Be comfortable. This usually means sitting. Adopt

whatever posture is best for you, so that you can gaze into the Stane for a period of time without becoming uncomfortable. You can hold the box containing the Stane in the palm of your hand or you can rest it on a rock, or tree stump.

Sit, first of all, *with closed eyes* and meditate on what you wish to see. If you want to see a particular person, meditate on that person—see them as you best know them, or as you last saw them. Don't try to project them into a scene that you want to find out about. That will come naturally later, when you start gazing. If it is a place that you are concerned about, concentrate your thoughts on that place, for a few moments. If it is a situation, then see the people involved in the situation, but don't try to force their actions and reactions.

Once you have adequately visualized what you are wanting to know, *clear your mind*. This is not easy. In the practice of Trascendental Meditation you are given a mantra on which to concentrate, so that your mind will not wander off on anything else. This can be useful in that form of meditation, but such strictness is not necessary for skrying. Simply try not to think of anything in particular. If you become aware of thoughts coming into your head, immediately clear them. With practice you will find that you can do this and keep it up for some considerable time.

Gaze into the black glass of the Keek Stane. In a very short time you will become aware of "pictures"—of scenes appearing within the reflective surface. With crystal gazing, using a crystal ball, you will most often seem to see the ball filling with white smoke. After a while this dispurses and leaves behind a clear scene. You do not experience such "smoke" in the Keek Stane. From the blackness of the glass you are suddenly aware of what could almost be taken for a miniature television picture. The scene is often dark at first, but with time—and practice—it will brighten. It is invariably in color and usually moving, rather than being a stationary photograph-like picture. It is, or should be, the very thing that you focused on just before starting to skry.

You do not have to gaze without blinking. Just relax and look into the Stane. Once the picture is there it will stay until you have seen all that is important, then it will slowly fade. Don't try to force it to return. Put away the Stane and take a rest.

However, it is possible, when you are well practiced, to change scenes—to focus on one thing and then, as your mind wills it, to shift to focus on something else. Don't be disappointed if you cannot do this right away. It does take a lot of practice. Through the Keek Stane it is possible to look into the future, the present, or the past. You program where and what you want to see by the meditation you do at the start.

The PectiWita use the Keek Stane a great deal. Through constant use, most become very proficient with it and would not be without it. A word of warning: don't use the Stane for more than twenty minutes at a time. It can become very tiring, though you may not be aware of that until you stop. If you keep going for too long you will be very drained when you end. This is a good time to seek out a tree and sit and draw energy from that nature-sibling.

## FIRE DIVINATION

Another way to divine, often used when the Keek Stane is not available, is through the flames and the embers of a fire. Once a good fire has been started, throw on some small branches of juniper and cedar, plus a few chips of sandalwood. It's good to have cut these yourself, with your Dirk. It is also said to be better if the original fire is started with "old" wood—gathered fallen tree limbs and/ or wood from old buildings, etc.—rather than freshly chopped logs.

Walk three times deiseil around the fire with your Staff, the end of it pointing into the fire, directing *maucht* into it. Then sit and make yourself comfortable. By gazing into the flames generated by the juniper, cedar, and sandalwood, you will be able to divine, just as you did with the Keek Stane after your initial meditation. If you can find one large flame to concentrate on, initially, it will help. You will also be able to "see" scenes in the glowing embers, as the fire dies down. These will not all be clear in that many will need to be studied and interpreted, to make sense of them. Sometimes you will see actual people and things, sometimes symbols, sometimes just letters and/or numbers. If the fire should die down too much, throw a little salt or sugar onto it and the flames will spring up again.

Write down everything you see, both in the fire and in the Keek Stane. This way, if you cannot think of what is meant by symbols shown to you at that moment, you may be able to place them later on.

There were innumerable signs and portents seen in the everyday domestic fire, in Scottish Highland life. For example, the sight of a seemingly hollow rectangular cinder falling from the other embers meant that there was a death coming (the cinder representing a coffin). A round cinder meant a birth (i.e. a cradle), and a perfectly square cinder a cashbox (money coming). If the fire suddenly blazed up it meant a visitor. A floating piece of ash, being carried up in the smoke, indicated a coming journey. A little fire magick was also done by the *semple* (the common people). On the night of a full moon they would write their desires on a piece of paper and cast it onto the fire. As the paper caught alight it would be carried up the chimney and the ashes would go out and be scattered.

To the Picts, the most sacred form of fire was the need-fire, produced by rubbing two pieces of wood together. The ritual kindling of the need-fire was one of the main ceremonies of the great festivals. As McNeill says:

> It was the most potent of all charms to circumvent the powers of darkness, and was resorted to in any immanent or actual calamity, or to ensure success in any important undertaking.

The simplest way to start a need-fire was to use two sticks; one with a point to it and the other with a hole into which the first stick would fit snugly. The stick with the hole lays on the ground and the pointed end of the other is inserted into it. The Witan then rapidly twirls the upright stick between his hands to cause friction and produce a spark. This form of firestarting was used in the islands of Skye, Mull and Tiree. Aidan Breac prefers a slightly more mechanical method, which I describe fully in the chapter on survival.

## THE EARTH SPEAKS

There is a form of divination, done by the PectiWita, using the earth itself and stones or pebbles from it. Find or make a clear patch of soil. Smooth it so that you have about a two foot diameter, flat circle. Gather twelve small stones. Some Witans gather these over a period of time and then keep them in a pouch, for divination purposes. But you can just pick them up for the particular casting you are going to do and then throw them away again afterwards. They should be about the size of marbles.

With your Dirk, or the point of your Staff, mark a straight line in the soil, dividing the area in half: | . Then mark three lines horizontally across this one: ≡≣

Cup the stones in your hands and breathe, or blow, onto them. Again, this is putting your *maucht* into the objects. Interestingly, this is where the act of gamblers blowing on their dice before rolling them comes from. Concentrate on the question you wish answered and throw the stones onto the ground. Now you must interpret the patterns of the stones.

The three lines across the center are to give you an idea of time. The closest to you is near the present; the middle one the near future, the furthest one the far future. Or you can think of them in terms of weeks, or months—however you want to interpret; whatever feels right for that time of casting the stones. The closer the stones are to the central line, the closer what you see will affect you. If they land on the far edges of the area then they will only have a passing effect on you (or whomever you are divining for).

The patterns can be read in various ways. Some basics are as follows:

Three or more in a line—a Journey; Travel

A line met by one or two—a Blockage

A curved line—Delay

Open Arrowhead—Rapid Advance

Inverted Arrowhead—Setback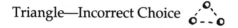

Triangle—Incorrect Choice

Inverted Triangle—Decision to be Made

Square—Stability

Diamond—Flexibility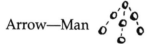

Arrow—Man

Inverted "Y"—Woman

It can be seen that there is a similarity here to tealeaf reading. You can certainly bring your psychic senses to bear and interpret according to how you feel. This can be a very good, quick way of getting the answer(s) to a simple question.

## AUGURY

The practice of augury was originally a system of checking with the gods to see whether or not the actions you contemplated would meet with their approval. For example, if you were thinking of doing an early planting of your crops because of unseasonal good weather, but then saw a squirrel carrying a nut into his hole, you would realize, through the squirrel's actions, that the gods were telling you "Winter is not yet over"!

Aidan Breac passed on some local beliefs along these lines, mostly dealing with birds. The Pictish tradition states that you must be standing facing south when looking for such signs. Breac suggests the Basic Stance with the Staff.

To see an eagle or a hawk circling deiseil is a positive sign. Circling widdershins, or tuaitheal (or "wranggaites"), is negative. The cry of a corbie (crow) or raven is favorable if coming from the right but not from the left. The hoot of an owl from the left, however, is good. Similarly pigeons and doves, seen or heard to the left are a favorable sign. Any bird actually flying, in a straight line, from left to right is positive; from right to left is negative.

To see an all white bird is a bad sign, sometimes a harbinger of death. Sighting a magpie means that news is coming, which could be either bad or good (the magpie being black and white), regardless of the direction it is flying. To see a swan is a bad sign, though that is offset if it is moving left to right. To hear a cuckoo is to expect good news.

If a deer suddenly bursts into the open, from cover, it is favorable if a doe but unfavorable if a buck. To see a running fox accompanied by pups is a sign of coming good fortune. To hear a frog croaking in the middle of the day means illness.

There are many other signs and portents, mostly associated with the weather, but these are a sampling of the ones indicating positive or negative influences.

## GO WITH THE WIND

I have mentioned the timing of magick, so far as the phases of the moon are concerned. And, as I said, this is really the only consideration that the PectiWitans take into account. However, for divination there is something else sometimes utilized: the wind. The Picts associated various attributes with the winds.

The East Wind was considered a benign wind. Probably because of the association with the rising sun, it was considered beneficial for workings (magick and divination) to do with new beginnings. Also for changes, changes of course, enlightenment.

The South Wind was for strength and for arousing emotions. It could be purifying and cleansing.

The West Wind was associated with the sea. It, too, could be good for cleansing. But its major function was in the field of love and romance. Its gentleness was that of the loving mother. It was a tender, soothing wind.

The North Wind was for strength. It was for endings and for separations; for decision-making.

These properties of the winds could be incorporated into the working of magick, if they happened to be blowing in the right direction at the time you were planning on doing it. Similarly (and more often, with the PectiWita) they could be worked into the practice of divination.

How do you tell which wind is blowing? First of all find out in which direction it is blowing. This can be done by observing things like smoke rising from chimneys or from your fire. Or study the tops of very tall trees and see in which direction they are being blown. Flags flying will also show you the wind direction, as well as fields of wheat, corn or even long grass. Another way is simply to kick up some fine dust and observe the direction in which it settles. Probably the most basic way is simply to stick your forefinger in your mouth and wet it, then hold it up in the air. The side which feels cold is the side from which the wind is blowing.

But having found where the wind is blowing from, how do you know whether that is north, east, south, or west? Obviously if you know where the sun rises, or sets, you can tell. But if it is midday, or midafternoon, or similar, you can still tell. Hold your watch flat and turn it around till the hour hand points at the sun. Then bisect the angle the hour hand makes with the figure twelve on the watch. For example, if it is four o'clock in the afternoon, half way between the four and the twelve will be two. So the line from the center of the watch out to the two is the line you want. That line is due South. Incidentally, don't forget to allow for summer time.

If you don't have a watch, guess at the time of day (it will probably be close enough). Then imagine that hour hand pointing at the sun and imagine bisecting that angle. This would be a good test of your imagination! But it will give you a close enough approximation of direction good enough to tell which wind is blowing. In the Southern Hemisphere, turn the *twelve* to the sun and then bisect the angle between it and the hour hand, for south.

Another way of doing this is to lay your watch level and then hold a small twig or blade of grass over the center point, so that a shadow falls across the face. Turn the watch till that shadow lies over the hour hand. North is then the point halfway between the hour hand (as it then points) and the twelve.

For finding direction at night, of course, you can use the stars. The Plow, otherwise known as the Great Bear, or the Big Dipper, is an easily recognized constellation. The two stars on the end of it point to the North or Pole Star, which in turn is at the end of the handle of the Little Dipper, or Little Bear. Another easily seen configuration is

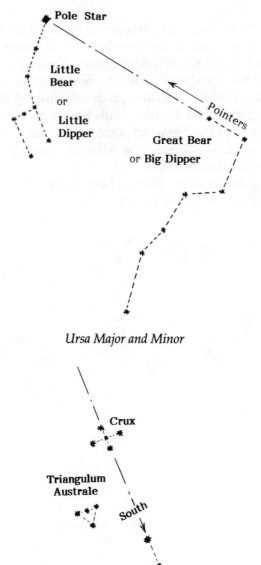

*Ursa Major and Minor*

*Southern Cross*

Orion, visible from all parts of the world (the Great Bear can only be seen in the Northern Hemisphere). If you draw a line up the center of Orion—through the center star of his belt and up through the center star of his head—and carry that line on through three more big stars, that third big star is the North or Pole Star. Very roughly, the three stars of Orion's sword point north. That line is north-south, of course, so can serve in the Southern Hemisphere to show the direction of south.

For the Southern Hemisphere, the Southern Cross is a good guide to where the south is.

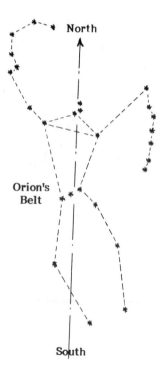

*Orion*

# 10. *Amulets and Talismans— Portable Power*

he belief in and use of talismans and amulets is found universally.

A TALISMAN is something—virtually anything can be used as a base—which has been magickally imbued with power and which can attract good fortune/protection and reject negativity. An AMULET, on the other hand, is something which *naturally* possesses those qualities.

The word "talisman" comes from the Arabic *tilsam*, plural: *tilsamên*, meaning "a magickal image." In *Man, Myth and Magic*, C. Nelson Stewart likens a talisman to a sword and an amulet to a shield, saying the former is a reinforcer and the latter a protector.

## *AMULETS*

One of the most common amulets, in the sense of being accepted as such among all races, is a stone with a natural hole through it. In Wicca, this is sometimes referred to, as a "hag stone" and is recognized as symbolizing the female genitalia. By virtue of this it is associated with the Goddess and, therefore, looked upon as having great positive power.

A hag stone can be carried in the pocket or hung, on a cord, around the neck. It should have been found in the wild by the person who will use it. In other words, if you simply purchase a hag stone from someone else, or from some supply house, it won't necessarily have the same efficacy as one you just happen to pick up off the ground. The hag stone is one amulet carried by most PectiWitans, though many have to search for years before finding one, depending on the region.

An elongated, phallic-like stone is equally appreciated by the Pictish Witches, as the masculine symbol of life. It is sometimes referred to as a "god stone." Both hag stone and god stone are protective amulets, protecting both from negativity and from disease.

On the island of Iona are found certain green pebbles. These are held in high esteem by the PectiWita, as protective amulets. They are also used by the local people and it is believed they can protect from drowning.

Since an amulet possesses its properties by virtue of what it is (or how it is shaped, as with the above two stones), it is really unnecessary to do anything to the object, such as cleanse and/or consecrate it. However, some people do feel they should do something. As with so much that is magickal, if you feel strongly enough about it—do it! So to consecrate something such as the hag stone I suggest simply washing it in the water of a running stream. (No soap! Simply hold it in the running waters.) Then hold it up in the light of the sun, turning it to all faces, to cleanse it.

The acorn is popular with Highland Witans. Symbol-

*Goddess Stone (or "Hag Stone") and God Stone.*

izing strength, it is good as a protective amulet and for imbuing the bearer with strength. I always carry an acorn
with me, in my pocket. I have also seen some beautiful
necklaces, made by stringing acorns together, that were
worn as especially potent amulets.

Although not particularly regarded by the PectiWita,
a generally popular amulet is the four-leafed clover. This
seems to be considered lucky simply because of its comparative rarity (yet the even rarer five-leaf clover is traditionally a symbol of *bad* luck!). Again, just to carry the
four-leafed clover with you is sufficient, it is believed, to
bring you "luck."

The mandrake root has, for centuries, been regarded
as magickal, if only because it grows naturally in human
shape. Even pieces of mandrake root are lucky. Again, it is
not something that the PectiWita particularly seek out, yet

many of them do carry a piece of the root. Similarly, High John the Conqueror root is a good amulet.

Aidan Breac taught his students to put more faith in what might be considered very ordinary items, but ones which were come by in extraordinary circumstances. For example, to find a bird feather is not too out of the ordinary. But to find a feather at the foot of a mountain that you are about to attempt to climb would have some significance (symbolizing the ability to rise up). So, under those circumstances, that particular feather could be regarded as a potent amulet for that occasion. It would behoove you to carry it with you to the top of the mountain.

Similarly, to discover a key lying on the ground at about the time that you are wondering about opening something—a business, a love affair, a new venture—would indicate that the key could be a strong amulet. And in this instance it would be an amulet, rather than a talisman. Although not a natural object, like a stone or nut, it is an amulet because of the circumstances of its finding. It is not something that has been especially made, and had power put into it through ritual, as would be the case with a talisman.

### TALISMANS

The Egyptians were great believers in, and users of, talismans. In *How To Make an Easy Charm to Attract Love Into Your Life* (Llewellyn 1990), Tara Buckland says:

> Egyptian magick relied primarily on the use of amulets, charms, magickal figures, pictures and formulas/chants. The Egyptians used magick as a cure for a great variety of problems: for protection from storms, wild animals, illness, wounds, poisons, and even ghosts...(They) had amulets and charms for everything. Many of these, such as the ankh and the

scarab, became very well known and have remained powerful symbols down through the centuries even into our own culture.

The four most common ancient Egyptian talismans were (1) those inscribed with the figure of Serapis, used to preserve against evils inflicted by earth, (2) those inscribed with the figure of Canopus, against evil inflicted by water, (3) those inscribed with a Hawk, against air, and (4) those with an Asp, against fire.

Talismans, Egyptian and other, are made on a wide variety of materials. They can be engraved or etched into metal; scratched into bone; carved into wood; drawn on parchment or paper. Short term ones—those needed for a specific purpose of short duration—are more likely to be done on paper, parchment, or perhaps even wood. Long term ones—such as for love or health—would more likely be done on metal or stone.

A good example of a talisman is the "Lee Penny" belonging to the Scottish Lockhart family. This is the coin that inspired Sir Walter Scott's story *The Talisman*. There is a long history of people being cured of illness through the agency of the Lee Penny. The usual method is simply to dip the coin into a goblet of water and swirl it around three times (deiseil, interestingly), then have the sick person drink the water. Sir Simon Locard of Lee obtained the talisman in the fourteenth century. He had taken an Emir prisoner and the coin was part of the ransom paid by the Emir's mother. She explained its properties to Sir Simon, and the method of using it. The coin is actually a silver groat with a dark red triangular-cut carnelian set into its center. It is claimed that it has the power to stop bleeding and cure fever and disease, in both humans and animals.

Healing has been a common use for talismans for

generations. I will talk more about this in Chapter Thirteen.

In High Magick, where everything must be done so exactly, talismans must be made of a certain metal, made at a certain time, consecrated at a certain hour, and so on. The sigils (signs) engraved on them are specified and everything has to be mathematically exact. Pictish Witchcraft is much more basic; much more accessible to the everyday person.

## PECTIWITAN TALISMANS

PectiWitan talismans are usually done on stone or wood. Stones are painted and wood is painted, carved or burned. The Witan will search for a suitable stone or piece of wood, or may just "happen" to come across one. This is then washed in a stream and dried in the sun. Signs are painted, carved, or burned onto it, appropriate for its purpose. Here, as with so much in PectiWita, Aidan Breac encouraged improvization. "Think about the purpose of the talisman," he would say. "Think about it carefully. Then decide what symbols would best portray that purpose."

Here are some symbols that have been used on PectiWitan talismans:

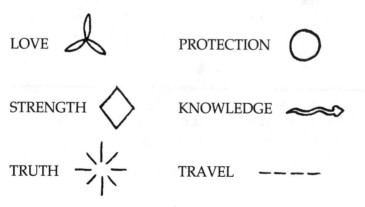

LOVE

PROTECTION

STRENGTH

KNOWLEDGE

TRUTH

TRAVEL

| MALE | | FEMALE | |
|------|---|--------|---|
| HOME | | WATER | |
| INCREASE | | DECREASE | |
| SUNRISE | | SUNSET | |
| HEALTH | | WEALTH | |
| DEISEIL | | WIDDERSHINS | |

Sometimes two or three symbols can be combined. For example, to strengthen and protect love, the three symbols would be superimposed on one another:

Once the symbols have been placed on the object, then you should cup it in your hands and concentrate your energies, your *maucht*, into it, thinking particularly of the purpose for which it has been made. Then hold it in the smoke of a ritual fire (of the type prepared for consecrating your working tools—see Chapter Five), thoroughly censing it, and finally hold it up in the light of the sun. It should then be carried, or worn, by the person it is for.

A number of Scottish families possess amulets and talismans that have been passed down, in the families, for generations. The Stone of Ardvorlich is possessed by the Stewarts of that name. It is an egg-shaped rock crystal set in four silver hoops. Legend has it that it was the badge of office of an ancient Arch-Druid. It is used much like the Lee Penny—dipped into healing water. The Stone of the Standard, or *Clach na Bratach*, is also a healing stone. It is a crystal that adhered to a clod of earth that stuck to a standard when it was drawn out of the ground at Bannockburn. The standard was that of the Chiefs of Clan Donnachaidh. Other famous stones include the Glenorchy Charm Stone (rock crystal), Keppoch Charm Stone (rock crystal), the Barbreck Bone (a piece of ivory), the Auchmeddan Stone (a black ball of flint mounted in silver), the *Clach-Bhuai* of the Campbells of Glenlyon, and the *Leug*, or Charm Stone of the Macleans.

One talisman that all PectiWitans make is the Witch's Protection Talisman, often referred to as the "Witch's Bottle." Once this has been made and deposited the individual need never worry about any negativity that may be directed in his or her direction, for such would be reflected back on the sender immediately, through the agencies of the bottle. To make one is simple.

Take a small bottle or jar and half-fill it with sharp objects—old nails, screws, pins, needles, bits of broken glass, etc. Then urinate in the bottle to fill it. A spot of your blood in there (menstrual blood is good for women to use) will give it added power. Put on the lid and fasten it with something like duct-tape or wax. Then bury the bottle at least nine inches deep, somewhere where you know it will not be disturbed. So long as it remains undisturbed, it will keep working for you. If you ever have any doubts as to whether or not it may have been accidentally dug up by someone, simply make another. Some Witans make one a year, just to be safe. With this sort of protection you need not worry about building "circles of white light," or any other protective devises; as I've said, you will always be protected.

## *THE SEVEN KNOT CHARM*

Another popular PectiWitan charm is the Seven Knot Talisman. This is made following the pattern of working magick described in Chapter Seven. Take a piece of cord, ribbon, of wool, about twenty-one inches long. If you like you may be guided by color symbolism and use the appropriate color cord (e.g. red or pink for love; green for health—see my book *Practical Color Magick*). *Very loosely*, tie seven knots along the length of the cord. They should be roughly equidistant but don't have to be exactly spaced. Concentrate on the purpose of the talisman as you tie them. Now start working yourself up to produce the *maucht* needed in magick. As you reach a high point, suddenly tug one of the knots tight. Continue working up, and tightening knots, till all have been tightened. You now have a potent talisman with real power tied into it. Again, cense it in the smoke of the fire, and then carry it with you at all times.

Sir James Frazer, in *The Golden Bough* (1890), mentions a Scottish cure for a sprained leg or arm is to cast nine knots in a black thread round the suffering limb, while you say:

> *The Lord rade,*
> *And the foal slade;*
> *He lighted*
> *And he righted,*
> *Set joint to joint,*
> *Bone to bone,*
> *And sinew to sinew.*
> *Heal, in the Holy Ghost's name!*

Frazer goes on to say, "This is a Christianized version of a very ancient spell for curing a lame horse. It was based on an incident in the myth of the Norse god Balder." In fact, in the original it starts: "Baldur rade; The foal slade ..." and ends "Heal! In Odin's name."

Frazer also tells of "a man in one of the Orkney Islands who was utterly ruined by nine knots cast on a blue thread." Pliny writes that some folk cured diseases of the groin by taking a thread from a web, tying seven or nine knots in it, and then fastening it to the patient's groin. A modern Arab cure for fever is to tie a cotton thread, with seven knots in it, around the wrist of the patient, who must wear it for seven days.

Since red is the color of blood, a large number of talismans are colored red for strength, health and protection. Many Highlanders make, and wear, necklaces of red rowan berries, or of red coral. Rowan twigs are tied together, with red thread, in the form of an equal arm cross, or a cross within a circle—symbolizing the sun—and placed over the door of the house. On the Quarter Days, especially, rowan twigs were placed over the entrance to the house.

F. Marian McNeill (*The Silver Bough*) speaks of charms of colored thread,

> Amber or "lammer" beads strung on red silk were frequently worn as an amulet by women of the upper

classes . . . Blue thread was also used as a charm, and was worn as a preventive by women liable to ephemeral fevers while suckling infants. These threads were handed down from mother to daughter and were esteemed on account of their age. Witches had their 'blue clews' . . . and "Winning the Blue Clew" is a well-known Hallowe'en rite.

## CHARGING THE STAFF

The Staff can also act as a magickal capacitor. You can do a ritual, much as described in Chapter Eight, to raise the *maucht*, but with no specific object in mind; just for the raising of the power. But instead of releasing it, direct it into the Staff by blowing "into" the thick end of it, as was done at its consecration (Chapter Five). The energy will then remain there until it is needed.

When needed, you again work up your power as in Chapter Eight, this time with your particular focus for it. When you feel the *maucht* is at its highest peak, point the Staff in the necessary direction, or into the center of the fire, and release both the power within you and that within the Staff, at the same time (*willing* it out, *shaking* it out and *shouting* it out). This is in the nature of "super-charging" your *maucht*. In this way you are able to send out a greatly enlarged dose to make happen whatever you will.

# 11. Song and Dance

ancing is a natural means of inducing religious or prophetic excitement, in many cultures. For example, such ceremonies as rain-making and crop-growing are frequently carried out by imitating the actions through which the gods bring the rain, or cause the rise of the grain. The dancers engage in a pantomimic dance to show the gods what it is they wish. Many times there is a mythical tale of how, "in earlier times," a god or supernatural being instructed the people in the details of this ceremony.

In *Wicca* (Llewellyn, 1988) Scott Cunningham, speaking of music, dance and gesture, says: "These techniques are used to raise power, alter consciousness and to unite with the Goddess and the God—to achieve ecstacy." That is precisely what song and dance do. In Chapter Seven I spoke of power-raising by *movement*; by rhythmically moving the body, slapping and/or clapping, and moving the feet. The way in which this can raise the *maucht* and, in particular, bring on ecstacy is well demonstrated in Voodoo rituals. There the object of the ecstatic dancing is specifically to bring about possession; for the worshippers to be "ridden by the loa" (possessed by the gods). This type of thing is found in many societies, primitive and not so primitive. To quote Lewis Spence: "Rhythmic motion appears to be inalienable from the fervour of primitive religious excitement. From the swaying movements of the body which accompany prayer in primitive and even in some modern religious castes it is, in more senses than one, merely a step to the general movement of the entire body in the dance." (*Myth and Ritual In Dance, Game and Rhyme*. London, 1947)

Ritual dance is certainly popular in the Highlands and Lowlands of Scotland. Much of it can be traced back to early religious and magickal ritual. For example, there are dances performed at St. Kilda, to celebrate the close of the fishing season. There is the Scottish "Ring Dance," performed in the Lowlands at the *Kirn*, or festival of the harvest, and usually done on the side of a hill to the sound of the Lowland bagpipe. There is the well-known Sword Dance, or *Gillie-callum* (so-called from the tune which accompanies it), performed over two drawn claymores. In Shetland the ritual which accompanies the Sword Dance bears a close resemblance to the Lowland drama of "Galatian," according to Spence. This can be traced to a death-and-resurrection folk drama of Keltic origin.

## SOLO DANCE

It is only in relatively recent times that we have had the proliferation of male/female couple dancing, as a form of social or "fun" dancing. Ancient dance would be either group, with all the males dancing together and/or all the females dancing together, or solo. Seldom, if ever, would you find a mix of males and females dancing.

Dance for the PectiWitan follows the old, traditional solo pattern.

The Pictish Witch will use dance to induce *ekstasis*, as I have mentioned. Simple, extemporaneous steps that do not have to be concentrated upon; that give rhythmic movement without demanding concentration . . . this is the type of dancing done for magick.

And it can also be done for celebration. The festivals—which I will look at in the next chapter—are times for celebration, for fun and merriment. Many Witans are drawn to express themselves in dance, and this can be extremely gratifying. Aidan Breac encouraged his students to include dance as part of ritual, as was done in ancient times. Apart from the use of it to raise *maucht*, it can also be used as an integral part of a longer ritual, for whatever purpose.

## DANCE STEPS AND RHYTHM

Although gesture is an integral part of dance, and important as a component of ritual, it is the footwork that needs to be concentrated upon by most newcomers to dance. I have stressed the extemporization, yet you need some idea of the basics before you can extemporize!

As an exercise, get a rhythm going in your head—a basic dum-dum-dum-DUM; dum-dum-dum-DUM; dum-dum-dum-DUM will do to start. Now just shuffle around in a circle, matching your steps to that rhythm. You will find that the final "DUM" calls for a solid stamp, so you'll find yourself doing a "shuffle-shuffle-shuffle-STAMP; shuffle-shuffle-shuffle-STAMP." This can be a good basic beat. But try others. Dum-DUM-dum; dum-DUM-dum; dum-DUM-dum will give you the stamp on alternate feet, which can make a nice change.

Start at a slow pace and then gradually increase your speed.

You can make your rhythm and steps as simple or as complex as you wish. A form of dancing known as "Step Dancing" is popular in the Highlands (and also with the English Gypsies, as it happens). It looks a little complicated at first but once you get the feel it can be very effective. Webster's defines it as "A dance in which steps are emphasized rather than gesture or posture; especially: a solo dance characterized by clogging, tapping, brushing or kicking." In *Sports and Pastimes of the People of England* (London, 1845), J. Strutt offers an Anglo-Saxon picture of two men apparently stepping or springing from foot to foot in a crouching posture and clapping their hands. One of the points of step dancing is that the dancer is not trying to follow music but, rather, is using the music simply as a metronome, to give him the rhythm and beat.

In step dancing there are four basics:

TAP - A beat made by the ball of the foot, or the toe, striking the ground with the weight remaining on the other foot.

STEP - A beat made by striking the ground with the ball or toe of the foot and taking the weight onto that foot.

HEEL DROP - Lowering the heel to finish with the weight distributed over the whole foot.

HOP/SPRING - Hopping/springing off the ground, landing either on the same foot (hop) or on the opposite foot (spring). In the spring the body weight is thereby transferred from one foot to the other.

Using these basics, with a little practice you can develop quite a variety of dance movements suitable for developing *maucht*. The main thing to remember, however, is that you want to be able to dance more or less without thinking; without having to concentrate on what steps you are taking. The purpose of the dance is to create movement and to build up the power within you.

Throughout England and Scotland ancient dance and ritual is kept alive by the Morris dancers and other traditional country dancers. There are such performances as the Horn Dance at Abbots Bromley, the Guise Dance in Cornwall, the Furry Day Festival in Padstow, Grose Dancing in the Scilly Isles, the Burry Man (or "Jack in the Green") in Edinburgh, and the many Robin Hood dances and Maypole dances. "Sides" (teams) of Morris dancers are active throughout the year, across the length and breadth of Great Britain, dancing the ancient patterns and keeping alive the old traditions.

### FOCUS—Sùil Dhè Mhóir

*Sùil Dhè Mhóir* ("The Eye Of the Great God") is the name given to the Pictish symbol used as a focus for dance ritual. There is a parallel here with the *vévé* of Voodoo. A symbol is drawn on the ground. It is scratched into the earth, or the grass, with the Staff or with the Dirk. Originally I'm sure it was one of the old Pictish "Crescent and V-Rod" sigils. There are many of these depicted in *The Early Christian Monuments of Scotland* by J. R. Allen and J. Anderson (Edinburgh, 1903). Aidan Breac gave his students five basics, but suggested that they go more with their own inner feelings and improvise for the specific purpose of the ritual. This basic five was:

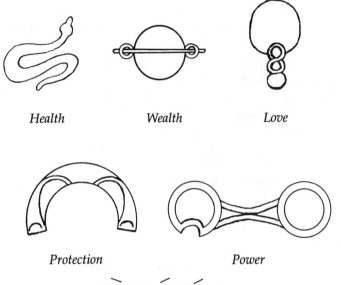

Health　　　　　Wealth　　　　　Love

Protection　　　　　　　　Power

SÙIL DHÉ MHÓIR

When the sigil has been drawn, the Witan should start his, or her, dance around the outside of the design, dancing deiseil. Dance around, slowly building up and moving faster. When you feel you are getting close to your climax, start to move in towards the center, now treading on the *Sùil Dhè Mhòir* and, as you continue dancing, treading it into the ground, as I detailed in Chapter Eight.

A final word on dance. Let me re-emphasize, it doesn't matter how casual or how choreographed your steps are. But as with most magick, simple is better. The dance is just a tool to help you work up to that state of ecstacy, to the "getting out of yourself." So don't worry how you look—no one is going to see you!

## WORDS AND SONG

Lewis Spence suggests "Folk-rhymes and some nursery rhymes are frequently survivals of myth—that is, they represent, in a broken-down or corrupted form, the spoken word or verbal description of rite, or otherwise retain some mythological memory."

> *Arthur o' Bower has broken his bands,*
> *And he's come roaring owre the lands;*
> *The King o' Scots and a' his power*
> *Canna turn Arthur o' Bower.*

The words of this old Scottish song refer to the wind, which has the seemingly unusual name of "Arthur o' Bower." The ancient British god Arthur was a god of the firmament and of the sun. Most gods of the sun are also wind gods. Spence suggests that "Bower" is a corruption of the Scots' word *bowder*, meaning a blast or squall of wind. Such a song might well have originally been sung as a magickal chant to conjure up the wind, or as part of an agricultural ritual of some type.

There are records of other Scottish pagan and Witan songs. One of the best known is that which was sung by the Berwick Witches as they danced a reel:

> *Cummer gae ye afore, cummer gae ye,*
> *Giff ye winna gae afore, cummer let me,*
> > *Ring-a-ring a-widdershins*
> > *Linkin' lythly widdershins*
> *Cummers carline crone and queyn*
> > *Roun' gae we!*
>
> *Cummer gae ye afore, cummer gae ye,*
> *Giff ye winna gae afore, cummer let me,*
> > *Ring-a-ring a-widdershins*

> *Loupin', lichtly, widdershins*
> *Kilted coats and fleein hair*
> *Three times three.*
>
> *Cummer gae ye afore, cummer gae ye,*
> *Giff ye winna gae afore, cummer let me,*
> *Ring-a-ring a-widdershins*
> *Whirlin', skirlin', widdershins*
> *And deil tak the hinnermaist*
> *Whae'er she be!*
> (Chambers' Journal, *April 1939*)*

According to the records of the trial of the Berwick Witches, there were some two hundred of them who went

> ... with flaggons of wine, making merrie and drink-
> ing ... to the Kirk of North Barrick, in Lowthian, and
> that after they had landed, tuk handes on the lande,
> and daunced this reill, or short daunse, singing all
> with one voice. One Geillis Duncan did goe before
> them, playing this reill upon a small trumpe.

An interesting point here is that they were dancing widdershins, or counterclockwise, rather than deiseil. The reason, apparently, was that they were specifically trying to work *negative* magick, at the behest of the Earl of Bothwell, aimed against King James VI of Scotland.

The song of a festival in Midlothian—where the dancers dance deiseil—describes how the merrymakers' intention is "to fetch the summer hame." There is also an ancient Scottish dance known as "Gillatrypes," which was supposedly performed by Witches. It came to be popular in Morayshire though the clergy claimed that the song

---

* Only the first two lines of this are given in most records of the trials. In her book *Hallowe'en*, F. Marian McNeill claims that she was actually responsible for the balance of it, as I give it above.

that accompanied it was "obscene"! "In a couple of days it was heard from the lips of all the youths and damsels in the streets," says J. M. McPherson (*Primitive Beliefs in the North-east of Scotland*, 1929).

There were many seasonal songs, particularly at May Eve. In many parts of Scotland the children would go house to house through the village, distributing garlands and singing:

> *A garland gay we bring ye here;*
> *And at your door we stand;*
> *It is a sprout well budded out,*
> *The work of our Lady's hand.*

According to Otta F. Swire (*The Outer Hebrides and Their Legends*, Edinburgh, 1966), in North Uist, off the northwest coast of Scotland, there was a celebration called "Carrot Sunday." This was on September 28th, the eve of St. Michael's Day. The females of the village would gather wild carrots—forked ones being especially prized—and bring them back to the village. There they would give them to other women, or men, while singing:

> *Cleft fruitful, fruitful, fruitful,*
> *Joy of carrots surpassing upon me,*
> *Michael the brave endowing me,*
> *Bride the fair be aiding me,*
> *Progeny pre-eminent over every progeny,*
> *Progeny on my womb, progeny on my progeny,*
> *Progeny pre-eminent over every progeny.*

The recipient of the carrot would say, "Children and blessings upon you." There is mention of Bride, a fertility goddess, in the verse. Also of Michael, who was the Christianized pagan god Lugh. The day continued usually with much dancing and revelry.

Song is not used much by the PectiWita as a whole. It is more an individual thing. Some few Pictish Witches will sing songs of their own creation at the festivals, for example, or perhaps compose chants to be used with magick working. But many more do not use song or chant at all. Aidan Breac did suggest that his students try their hand at composition, but it was not mandatory.

> *Dance, dance;*
> *'Round the* gleede. *(glowing fire)*
> *Celebrate*
> *I' word and deed.*
> Semple *folk (common people)*
> *And* pibroch *sounds (bagpipe music)*
> *The* nicht *is long (night)*
> *And* kens *nae bounds. (knows)*
>
> —Aidan Breac

# *12. Festivals/ Celebrations*

ohn Gregorson Campbell makes an interesting comment, in his *Witchcraft and Second Sight In the Highlands and Islands of Scotland*. He says: "The notations of the Celtic year belong to the Christian period, old style. If there are any traces of Pagan times they are only such as are to be gathered from a few names and ceremonies." However, he goes on to say, "The four seasons are known as *earrach*, spring, *samhradh*, summer, *fogharadh*, harvest, and *geamhradh*, winter . . . There can be no doubt the origins of the names belong to a period anterior to Christianity."

Indeed *earrach* is derived from ear, meaning the head or front, also the east. *Samhradh* is from *samh*, the sun. Fogharadh is from *fogh*, meaning hospitality and abundance. *Geamhradh* is connected to *geamhtach*, meaning stiff, thick, binding, and thus seems tied-in with the idea of snow and ice.

The great world festivals originated in the worship of the sun and the earth-powers, according to F. Marian McNeill:

> In Europe there were two main festivals, which fell exactly six months apart, and each half year was again bisected and marked with a minor festival. But the dates of these festivals were not everywhere identical; for whilst the non-Celtic peoples divided the year in accordance with the solstices and equinoxes, with Midsummer Day and Midwinter Day, or Yule, as their chief festivals, the Celtic peoples divided it in accordance with the entry of the seasons, their two principle festivals being Bealltainn (1 May) and Samhuinn or Hallowmass (1 November) . . . The fire-festivals of the Celts coincided neither with the solstices and equinoxes nor, as we might have expected, with the two principle seasons of the agricultural year, the sowing in spring and the reaping in autumn.

But she points out that the dates of Bealltainn and Samhuinn, while unimportant to the European husbandman, did deeply concern the European herdsman. It was on the approach of summer that the herdsman drove his cattle out into the open to graze, but on the approach of winter that he brought them back to the shelter of the stall. Frazer says:

> Accordingly it seems not improbable that the Celtic bi-section of the year at the beginning of May and the beginning of November dates from a time when the Celts were mainly a pastoral people, dependent for subsistence on their herds.

With the Scottish Quarter Days differing from the English Quarter Days, McNeill concludes that "Scotland follows the ancient custom of the Celtic peoples, and England that of the non-Celtic peoples of Europe." The Scottish Quarter Days are as follows:

February 2 - Candlemas
May 15 - Whitsun, or Old Bhealltainn
August 1 - Lammas
November 11 - Martinmas, or Old Hallowmas

The ancient Keltic year started on the eve of November 1. Then, in 527 C.E., this was changed and New Year's Day was declared to be March 25. Almost a thousand year's later this was changed again, to January 1. In Scotland it wasn't until 1600 that New Year's Day was first celebrated on January 1. The PectiWita, in common with most Wiccans, still celebrate the start of the year at Samhuinn, though their Samhuinn is November 11 rather than November 1, as with much of Wicca.

In early, pre-Christian times people followed a basically lunar calendar. *Festival celebrations began at the rising of the moon. In other words, they started on the EVE of the actual day.* Celebration and festivities would then continue for a number of days—seven or more. In Scotland, and much of Europe, great bonfires would be kindled on hilltops on the Quarter Days. Then, in 46 B.C.E., the Romans switched from lunar reckoning to following the sun, and introduced the Julian calendar. In 1582 C.E. Pope Gregory XIII amended that to the Gregorian calendar, though well into the latter half of the nineteenth century Scottish country folk still celebrated their festivals according to the "Old Style" reckoning. In fact, in some of the more remote parts of the Highlands the custom has still not entirely died out.

The calendar, festivals, customs, and celebrations can become very complicated, especially when you start studying the changes that have taken place over the centuries. But Aidan Breac felt that the PectiWita celebrated only those festivals/dates which were pertinent to them. These were:

*Samhuinn*—November 11
*Yule*—December 22 (*Feill Fionnain*)
*Bealltainn*—May 15
*Midsummer*—July 5 (*Feill-Sheathain*)

On the face of it this seems a mixture of both the Keltic and non-Keltic celebrations. Breac explained that the two main divisions of the year are there: the start of summer and the start of winter. Also there are the two most obvious solar divisions: the summer and winter solstices—the longest and shortest days of the year. Whilst other festivals might have been observed by various Pictish Witches at different periods (and some might still be today, on a personal basis), these are the four main "Sabbats" now celebrated by the PectiWita. The names used by the PectiWita are:

*Samhuinn*,
*Feill-Fionnain* (or Yule),
*Bealltainn*,
*Feill-Sheathain* (or Midsummer).

A large fire was a must for the Sabbat celebrations. Similarly, to be on the top of a high ben (hill or mountain), was preferred. Until relatively recent times fires could always be seen burning on the tops of mountains scattered right across Scotland, on the festival dates. In *Primitive Beliefs In the North-East of Scotland* (London, 1929) J. M. McPherson says: "[The fire] destroyed the powers hostile to man, purified the air, and allowed man and beast and vegetation to thrive and become fertile."

As we know, the PectiWita is a solitary tradition, so even the Sabbats are celebrated by individuals rather than by large groups. But occasionally you will find two or three PectiWitans joining together in the rites at these times, if they happen to be in contact with one another and feel so inclined. (Similarly, at Sabbat *and* Esbat, you may well find husband and wife joining together.)

Highlanders and Lowlanders alike love to party, so the Sabbat periods are frequently celebrated by Witan and non-Witan alike, often without the latter's knowledge of the true cause for celebration! After the ritual work, a Pictish Witch might well descend from the ben and get together with friends (Witan and non-Witan) to kill a few bottles of McEwans or Glenfiddich or the like!

## SAMHUINN
## November 11

Pronounced "Sow-un" ("Sow" to rhyme with "doe"). This is the start of the year and the start of winter. This, then, was a time when thoughts were on the Horned God who oversaw the hunt in earlier days, for this was the time when humankind had to go back to hunting animals for food, to get through the winter.

The fire is lit as the sun starts to go down and the Samhuinn ritual starts as the moon ascends the sky; as previously stated, on the eve of Samhuinn. Have plenty of wood available beside the fire, for you will want to keep the fire burning through the night. Make sure there is wine or ale in your Quaich and that there is Mool (a bowl of earth) available.

Standing in the east and facing east, back to the fire, hold your Staff with both hands horizontally above your head. Breathe deeply and feel the energy of the moon flowing in, filling and cleansing your body. Then lower the Staff, assume the Basic Stance, and Center.

Walk three times around the fire, deiseil, holding the Staff to point in to the center of the fire. Back at the east, once more raise the Staff in both hands above your head and shout:

*A null e; A nall e; Slàinte!*

Lower the Staff and lay it on the ground. Facing the fire, take out your Dirk and hold it before you, blade pointing up. Say:

*As the long days of summer draw to a close I call upon the gods to watch over me through the dark*

*days of winter. Great God, see that my belly is full
and that I have warmth and shelter when I need it.
Keep me free of harm and give me the strength to help
others who may not fare as well as I do.*

Walk one quarter of the way around the fire (to the
south), moving deiseil, and repeat the above prayer. Then
move on to the next quarter (west) and repeat it. Finally
move to the fourth quarter (north) and repeat it. Return to
the east, where you started.

*A Samhuinn Evocation*

Take up a piece of wood and, with your Dirk, sharpen the end of it so that it becomes a stake. With both hands, stick this stake into the ground at the edge of the fire. (If necessary, pound in the stake using a rock.) If the whole area is too stony for you to be able to stick the wood into the ground, then simply lay it down with the sharpened end pointing in towards the fire.

Move around to the south and repeat this. Do it again at the west and the north. Then take the Quaich, filled with wine or ale, and circumambulate once more. This time pour a little of the wine/ale around the base of each stake. When you arrive back at your starting point, take a drink from the Quaich.

Standing again in the east, take up your Staff. Place its base close against the first stake, holding the Staff at the top with both hands. Say:

> *Here have I planted four sturdy trees. May they provide me with fuel to warm me and cook my food through the dark days of winter. As with all life, let me not take more than I need for my immediate survival.*

Move to the north and sit. Take the Mool and place the bowl between your legs so that you can sit with the fingers of both hands dug lightly into the earth.

Samhuinn is a time when the veil between the worlds is thin. It is therefore a time when you may make contact with those who have died. Close your eyes and once more breathe deeply and Center yourself, feeling your body attuning itself to the earth and all that it contains.

As we discussed in Chapter Three, all things merge together in a web of spirit, at the base level of existence. In this way it is possible to make contact with animals, plants, and even minerals. Also in this way it is possible to contact the spirits of those who have died. By allowing your mind to sink down into the basic levels, and to go out across the network of life that is there, you may make contact with whomever you wish.

Sit, then, and send out your thoughts in a search for the one you wish to contact. Think of them as you best knew them, but see them happy and healthy. See them as they would probably want to see themselves. It may take a while to make contact. Don't try to rush it . . . you have all night if necessary! But eventually you *will* make contact. You will be able to "converse" with the one you sought. If you have no desire to communicate with anyone in this way then, of course, this section may be omitted.

At the end of your time, when you have bidden farewell and thanked the gods for the contact, breathe deeply, open your eyes and allow yourself to come back to your surroundings. Stand and, walking around the fire, scatter the soil from the bowl.

Take up your Staff and face west. Raise it horizontally above your head, holding it with both hands. Shout:

A null e; A nall e; Slàinte!
*Welcome to the new year!*
*May it teach me as well as did the old.*
A null e; A nall e; Slàinte!

The ritual is over. Most Witans stay at the fireside till dawn, either in meditation or sleeping. If two or three Witans have come together to celebrate, they would surely party! And, as mentioned above, there would usually be general celebration in the villages and towns at the times of the Sabbats. Since this particular ceremony marks the start of a new year, in many parts of the Highlands household fires are extinguished and then the first fire of the new year is kindled from a piece of wood taken from the Samhuinn ritual fire.

Many of the games associated with the old New Year have now been transferred to the new New Year (January 1), but PectiWitans still play them on the original November date.

In Lewis and South Uist, on New Year's Eve, the head man of a village would wrap the hide of the *mart* or winter cow (a cow killed for winter use) around his head and make off, followed by all the other men. The men would beat at the cowhide, with switches, making a noise like a drum. According to J. G. Campbell:

> The disorderly procession went three times *deiseil*, according to the course of the sun, round each house in the village, striking the walls and shouting on coming to a door:

> "The *calluinn* (pelting) of the yellow bag of hide,
> Strike the skin (upon the wall)
> An old wife in the graveyard,
> An old wife in the corner
> Another old wife beside the fire,
> A pointed stick in her two eyes,
> A pointed stick in her stomach,
> Let me in, open this."

> Before this request was complied with, each of the revellers had to repeat the rhyme though, as might be expected, when the door opened for one, several pushed their way in, till it was ultimately left open for all.

Once inside, the men were offered refreshments and the leader gave the head of the household the *Caiseinuchd*. This is a strip of skin from the heart of a sheep, which used to be ritually killed at this time of year. The fragment is oval in shape and, says Lewis Spence, "no knife must be used in removing it from the skin." This is wrapped around the point of a shinty stick and singed in the fire. It is then passed three times deiseil around the family, and held to the noses of all, for them to smell. It is a bad omen for the person in whose hand it ceases to burn. The *caisean-uchd* is regarded as a potent charm against evil. Not a drop of drink would be taken till this ritual had been done.

First thing in the morning of the New Year the head of the household, for luck, will treat everyone in the house to a dram of whisky and a spoonful of half-cooked *sughan* (pronounced "soo-an"), an ancient Keltic dish. The toast is *Bliadhna mhath ùr dhuit* ("A good New Year to you"), and the response: *Mar sin duit fhein is mòran diu* ("The same to you, and many of them").

"First-footing" is treated seriously. The very first person to enter the house on New Year's Day should be a dark-haired man bearing gifts of a piece of coal or peat, and/or salt and bread. Many households will not allow anyone to enter the house until the appropriate first-footer has come.

New Year's Day is a great *saining* day—a day for taking precautions against bad luck, both to the humans and to the animals of the household. Juniper was burned in the byre; the house was decked with mountain ash; door-posts, walls, even cattle, were sprinkled with wine.

One of the methods of divination practiced by almost everyone on New Year's Day was to toss a shoe over the roof of the house. The shoe had to be held by the tip when thrown. The thrower would then rush around to the other side of the house to examine how the shoe had landed. It was believed that in whichever direction the toe pointed, that was a direction the thrower would be taking before long. However, if the shoe landed with the sole upper-most, this was a sign of misfortune to come.

## FEILL-FIONNAIN, or YULE
### December 22

The shortest day of the year and the longest night. At this time the sun rises and sets at its most southerly point. The day usually falls on December 22, though this will vary from year to year.

*Feill-Fionnain* means "Fionn's Eve," for the great Keltic god Fionn, or Finn (equated by some scholars with Lugh). Campbell says of him,

> There are very few Highlanders that cannot even now say something about Fionn and his heroes (the Feinne); how they fought and died . . . Rocks, hills and streams are called after the Feinne. Surnames are derived from them . . . the Feinne and their exploits pervade all Celtic Scotland and all Gaelic tradition.

Again, Yule is celebrated with a large bonfire on the top of a ben. Since it can be very cold (and frequently snowy), the fire is usually very much appreciated! As at Samhuinn, however, there is a sacredness about the fire. The main log in it—the largest—is the Yule Log. This must have been cut from the celebrant's own tree or have been a gift from a neighbor. It must not be a log that was bought. It is traditionally oak, ash or beech. In some areas of the Highlands the Pictish Witch will carve into the Yule Log the semblance of an old woman. This is known as *Cailleach Nollaich*, or the Yule Old Wife. A toast to future prosperity is drunk, from the Quaich, over the log before it is taken away to the ritual fire, and libations poured over it. At the start of the ritual the Yule Log stands to one side, to be placed on the fire at a particular point.

The ritual starts, as at Samhuinn, as the moon ascends the sky. Standing in the south, facing north and the fire, hold your Staff with both hands horizontally above your head. Breathe deeply and feel the energy of the moon flowing in and filling, and cleansing, your body. Then lower the Staff, assume the Basic Stance, and Center.

Walk once around the fire, deiseil, holding the Staff to point in to the center of the fire. Back at the south, once more raise the Staff in both hands above your head and shout:

*A null e; A nall e; Slàinte!*

Putting down the Staff, place the Yule Log across the center of the fire. Take up the Mool and hold it, in both hands, up to the sky. Say:

*Here is the sacred earth: that which sustains us all. In it we find the roots of life; the trees and plants. Beneath it and above it exists life. It is our footing and our foundation.*

Lower the Mool and hold it to your chest. Say:

*Though the earth be covered with a mantle of white, yet is it still our support. Now may the days grow ever longer. Now may the light shine forth from the sky, turning the tide of winter. Let the God march on towards the springtime. Let Him open the gates for the Lady to re-enter. Here I do burn the mighty Yule Log, to add strength to the Lord for the remainder of his journey. May He draw on it when in need.*

Raise the Mool once again. Say:

*Oh, Lord! You have carried me safely through this dark part of the year. Please bear me forward to its*

*ending. Plant my feet firmly on the way and let them
not drift nor slip from their intended direction.*

Carefully pour out the earth upon the ground in the
form of a simple Pictish "Crescent and V-Rod." Then take
your Quaich and drink a toast to the Lord and the Lady,
being careful not to drain the cup! Pour the rest of the wine
onto the sigil on the ground.

Keep the fire burning till the dawn.

*Crescent and V-Rod*

## BEALLTAINN
## May 15

May Day festivities were originally part of the general Bealltainn celebrations and the erection of Maypoles was a common practice. In *Earth Rites* (London, 1982) Janet and Colin Bord say:

> A general rather than specific acquisition of fertility was intended by the widespread use of trees and foliage in May Day celebrations throughout Europe. In the belief that the tree-spirit would fertilize women and cattle, and make the crops grow, houses and farm buildings were decked with greenery, while whole trees were cut and then re-erected in the village. Although later a pole was left permanently erected and then decorated at each year's May festivities, originally a new tree was brought each year. Since the tree embodies the newly awakened spirit of vegetation, a dead tree would hardly have the same power, and the re-use of a 'dead' pole indicated that by then the real meaning of the custom had been forgotten, although as a phallic symbol it could still suggest the flow of energy between cosmos and earth which the people were seeking to invoke.

The frequently orgiastic fertility festivities associated with Bealltainn were too blatant to be adopted by the Christian Church, which had assimilated so many Pagan practices. By 1644 the Puritans had got Parliament to ban May festivities and to do away with the Maypole. But with the return of Charles II in 1660, the people joyfully brought back their old beliefs and practices. On the first Bealltainn after Charles's return, a Maypole 134 feet tall was erected in the Strand and remained there until 1717.

As I have already pointed out, Bealltainn falls on the

old date of May 15. As with all the other PectiWita Sabbats, the ritual starts on the rising of the moon the night before. Have your Quaich available, filled with wine or ale. Also have a hard-boiled egg beside the Quaich. The Witan's Staff may be decorated with bright ribbons, greenery and wild flowers.

In this instance the ritual starts with the Witan standing in the west, facing the east and the fire. Hold the Staff, by its lower section, straight up in the air and shout:

*A null e; A nall e; Slàinte!*

Bearing the Staff, march three times deiseil around the fire as you chant:

*Plant the seeds on Bealltainn's Eve;*
*Let all earth awake!*
*The crops will grow, we do believe,*
*As man with woman mates.*
*This is the time for green to rise*
*And greet the Springtime sun.*
*This is the time for all of life*
*To join and grow as one.*

You can repeat this, if necessary, as you walk around. When you get back "plant" the Staff in the ground in front of you, either by sticking it into the earth or, if the ground is rocky, by simply holding it upright. Spend some time thinking of the joy of life; of seeds planted and beginning to sprout; of the act of love and creation; of the beginnings of all life.

Laying down the Staff take up the egg and hold it up, cupped in your hand, to the light of the moon. Say:

*Here is a beginning. Let me always respect and cherish life; to honor it in all things.*

Break away the shell of the egg, and continue:

*Life is ongoing. It bursts forth, out of its formative, protective shell, into the mainstream. There is much to learn and much to experience. Life should be a continuing, pleasurable cycle. Help me to learn by my experiences and thereby to progress. I here absorb this new life, remembering my own beginnings.*

Sit and eat the egg. Contemplate your early years; your struggles and joys. Think about where you want to go in your life. Redefine your goals and renew your dedication to achieving them.

If as occasionally happens the rite is being celebrated by a male and a female Witan together, then this is a wonderful time to make love. It is also, of course, a *traditional* time for love-making.

*A Bealltainn Toast*

The Witan(s) may now meditate or sleep till dawn. The Bealltainn fire should burn all night, as is usual at the Sabbats. When the first rays of the sun break the horizon, stand and raise your Dirk in your right hand and your Quaich in the left (*vice versa* if left-handed). Say:

A null e; A nall e; Slàinte!
*Welcome the Spring! Welcome back, my Lady!*
*The Lord has brought me through the darkness of*
    *winter.*
*The Lady greets me in the dawn of summer;*
*The wheel of the year turns and turns.*
*Once more the Lady is seated upon her throne.*
*Long may she reign! Long life to all life!*
Slàinte!

Drain the wine/ale from the Quaich and then kneel and stick the Dirk into the ground with another cry of "*Slàinte!*"

In some parts of Scotland what was once a great fire festival has degenerated into a children's game. Spence notes (*Myth and Ritual in Dance, Game, and Rhyme*):

That it had once been celebrated by adults is clear from earlier accounts of it. The remaining rite consisted of the placation of such animals as preyed upon the flocks and herds—eagles, foxes, and so forth—by casting sops of custard to them. That the ceremony had once included human sacrifice seems likely from the casting of lots for a possible victim with which it is connected. The custard, when hard baked, was cut into small portions, one of which was smeared with charcoal, and these were placed in a bonnet. Whoever drew the blackened portion, it was jestingly implied, was 'to be sacrificed to Baal' (the Celtic god Beli), whose favour was implored to render the year productive to man and beast.

Breac emphasizes the positive aspects of the time of year, stressing the Pictish Witches' concern for the continuation of life. Certainly the focus of the majority of Bealltainn rituals, Scottish and otherwise, is on the sowing of seeds and the fertility of all things.

## FEILL-SHEATHAIN, or MIDSUMMER
### July 5

July 5 is the date of Old Midsummer. *Feill-Sheathain* means "Swithin's Eve." Swithin is the old form of John, the common form being *Iain, Eoin,* and *Eathin*. Many ancient Pagan sites dedicated to Baldur were rededicated, by the Christian Church, to St. John the Baptist. Baldur was, of course, a radiant Sun god.

Throughout Scotland, and the rest of Britain, villagers would make "cartwheels" of straw and dip them in pitch. On Midsummer's Eve these would be set alight and bowled down hillsides, to give power to the sun god. If the flames went out before the wheel reached the bottom of the hill, it presaged a bad harvest. On the other hand, if the wheel remained burning brightly throughout its run, there would be an abundant harvest.

Torches are frequently lit from the ritual bonfire. In the Orkneys these torches, made primarily of heather, are then carried through the cowsheds to keep away sickness and to make the cattle fertile. In other parts of the country the torches are carried around the fields and the houses of the village, always moving deiseil.

The smoke of the ritual fire was also held in awe. To be censed by it ensured a healthy year to come. Mothers would hold their babies in the smoke of the Midsummer bonfire, to bless them. Jumping over the fire, as it blazed, was another time-honored custom. Highland women were prone to leap over the fire with their skirts held high, exposing their genitals to the smoke and flame, to bring fertility. Ashes from the fire were much sought after. Sprinkling them on the fields would ensure a good harvest. Ashes were rubbed on the foreheads of children to bless them and rubbed on genitals to ensure fecundity.

For the PectiWitan ritual, the Midsummer fire is kindled and plenty of wood is gathered to keep it going through the night. The Mool bowl is filled with fresh earth; the Quaich with wine or ale. Stand in the north, facing the south and the fire. Stand with the Staff beside you, in your right hand (left if left-handed). Breathe deeply, cleansing your body through the light of the moon. Then take the Basic Stance and Center yourself.

Hold the Staff horizontally, with both hands, above your head and say:

> A null e; a nall e; Slàinte!
> *Hail to the Sun God! Hail to the Lady!*
> *As the Goddess watches over our land and our crops,*
> *so does the God move on his destined way across the*
> *sky, reaching now the zenith of his journey.*

Choosing a time when the flames of the fire are not too high (!), run forward and leap across the fire to land in the south. You can (and most Witans do) use your Staff to "pole-vault" across, if you wish. On the other side, raise your Staff with both hands and cry: *"Slàinte!"* Turn and face the fire again.

Throw on more wood to allow the fire to blaze up. Say:

> *I here kindle the fire of the sun, giving strength to the*
> *Lord. May he and the Lady watch over me through*
> *these long days of summer. Let me enjoy the pleas-*
> *ures of life, as you have given it to me, but let me not*
> *abuse life in any form. I renew my pledge to your*
> *service and to the service of all life, in whatever form I*
> *meet it.*

Take up the Mool bowl and dip into it to sprinkle the earth onto the fire. Say:

> *The Earth relies upon the Sun for life. Here do I join earth with the heat and light of the sun. Let them together strengthen and fortify one another.*

With the wine, or ale, in your Quaich, toast the gods, and all (by name) who are special to you, wishing them long life and happiness. Toss the last of the wine onto the fire.

In the morning, when the fire has died, take some of the ashes and keep them for the coming months. They can be used as a powerful protective and strengthening agent on amulets and talismans and even on the human body. This applies to the ashes from each of the Sabbat fires.

For all of the above Sabbat rituals, "words from the heart" should be the rule. Read and understand the meaning, the sense, of what is given here. Then try to use your own words. The PectiWitan tradition is one of extemporization, as Aidan Breac repeatedly stated. Also, remember that incense can, and should, be used in your rituals. Either blended incense or, better yet, natural fumigants thrown directly onto the ritual fire.

As I have mentioned, although the PectiWita is a solitary tradition, it is not uncommon for couples in the sense of husband and wife, to work together.

# 13. *Herbal Lore and Healing*

ike most Wiccans, Pictish Witches have a good knowledge of herbs and are adept at healing, both through the use of herbs and by other methods. PectiWitans should certainly be able to administer to them–selves and their neighbors when sick.*

### *HERBS*

Most sicknesses experienced in any particular country can be cured by using things found growing in that country. To be prepared for any sickness, stock up on a number of basic herbs, flowers, barks and roots, carefully drying and then storing them for future use. Keep them packed in jars, or envelopes, ready for emergencies. One thing all Witans must remember, however, is to ask permission from the herb before cutting it. Ask permission to

---

\* The healing processes described in this and other chapters are those that have been used for generations by Scottish Witches. In no way do I wish to imply that they should be used over and above the services of a competent physician.

use it and explain how it will be used for healing purposes. Cut the herb with your Dirk.

Here are some of the leaves, flowers, barks and roots used by the Picts:

*LEAVES*

    Ash – for rheumatoid arthritis
    Blackberry – diarrhoea
    Blackcurrant – catarrh; sore throat
    Camomile – debility
    Dandelion – laxative; tonic
    Golden Rod – vomiting
    Ground Ivy – ulcers
    Horehound – coughs; beer–making
    Lobelia – bronchial complaints; croup
    Nettles – blood pressure; rashes
    Peppermint – flatulence
    Plantain – piles
    Raspberry – gargle for throat
    Rosemary – hair stimulant
    Sage (wood sage) – kidneys; liver
    Scabious – internal inflammation
    Sorrel – cooling, fever drink
    Southernwood – female disorders
    Sweet Chestnut – asthma; chest complaints
    Thyme – antiseptic
    Violet – poultices
    Wormwood – digestion; worms
    Yarrow – colds; fevers

*FLOWERS*

    Camomile – hysteria
    Elder (*Sambucus nigra*) – urinary problems
    Red Clover – coughs

Hop – stomach complaints
Marigold – promotes perspiration
Safflower – fevers; female complaints


## ROOTS

Burdock (*arctium lappa*) – blood purifier
Dandelion – rheumatics; liver complaints
Lily of the Valley – valvular disease of the heart
Male Fern – worms
Marshmallow – dysentery
Red Dock – blood purifier
Rhubarb – aperient (gentle laxative)
Solomon's Seal – pulmonary troubles


## BARKS

Alder (*Prinos verticillatus*) – aperient
Ash – laxative
Oak – antiseptic and tonic
Birch – eczema
Cherry – lung diseases
Willow (*Salix alba*) – rheumatic fever

A good basic way of using the above is to infuse one ounce of the herb, root or bark in one pint of water and then to take one wineglassful each morning and night. (1 wineglass = 1/16 pint)

The following are some recipes taken from Aidan Breac's personal book. Do not boil preparations in aluminum containers. Use copper, earthenware or glass.

Coughs, colds and chilblains seem to be common problems in and around the Highlands.

For COUGHS place 1/4 pint of white vinegar in a basin together with 1/4 oz. black licorice broken up and finely ground. Place over a gentle heat and stir until the licorice dissolves. Add 2 oz. honey, stirring well, and as it all cools add the juice of a lemon. *Dose:* 1 teaspoonful whenever the cough is troublesome.

Alternate recipe: Steep 3 oz. crushed Blood Root (*Sanguinaria canadensis*) in good vinegar for 2 weeks. Strain. Add 1-1/2 lbs. honey and gently simmer down to 2/3 volume. *Dose:* 1/2 teaspoonful when needed.

For CHEST COLDS soak 1 tablespoon of Althea Root, Leaves, and/or Flowers (*Althaea officinalis*) in 1/2 cup of cold water for 8 hours, to make "Althea Tea." Then, separately, thoroughly mix 2 oz. Lungwort (*Pulmonaria officinalis*), 2 oz. Coltsfoot Leaves (*Tussilago farfara*), and 1 oz. Anise Seed (*Pimpinella anisum*). Steep 2 teaspoonsful of this mixture in 1/2 cup of boiling water. Mix this with 1-1/2 cups of the Althea tea and add honey. *Dose:* 1 tablespoonful three times a day.

For CHILBLAINS use two pints of unsalted water in which parsnips have been boiled (but have been removed). Mix in 1 tablespoonful of powdered alum, stirring well. Bathe the feet or hands with the solution for twenty minutes. Allow the solution to dry on the skin before rinsing clean.

For SORE THROATS make a tea of 1 oz. Selfheal (*Prunella vulgaris*) to 1 pint water. *Dose:* 1 wineglassful 3 times a day.

A good GARGLE for sore throats can be made from Sumac leaves or bark, (*Rhus glabra*) made into a tea.

For HOARSENESS boil 1 oz. of blackcurrant leaves in one pint of water. Strain and bottle. *Dose:* 1 teaspoonful two or three times a day.

Another recipe for a SORE THROAT is to make a tea of Selfheal (*Prunella vulgaris*) using 1 oz. of the herb to 1 pint of water. *Dose:* a wineglassful drunk slowly two or three times a day.

Other general remedies include the following.

For ASTHMA mix equal parts Garlic (*Allium sativum*), Ground Ivy (*Nepeta hederacea*), Blackthorn (*Prunus spinosa*) and Blue Vervain (*Verbena hastata*). Take 4 teaspoonsful of the mixture and simmer in 1 qt water for 20 minutes. Strain. *Dose:* 3 tablespoonsful 3 times a day.

A poultice for ARTHRITIS can be made by mixing 9 parts Slippery Elm Bark (*Ulmus fulva*), 6 parts Mullein leaves (*Verbascum thapsus* or *V. nigrum*), 3 parts Lobelia (*Lobelia inflata*) and 1 part Cayenne (*Capsicum frutescens*). Add 3 oz. of the mixture to boiling water and form a paste. Spread this on a piece of cloth and apply to the afflicted area.

For BLADDER PROBLEMS boil 1 oz. of Parsley Piert (*Alchamilla arvensis*) in 1 pint of water for 1 minute, then cool and strain. *Dose:* 1 wineglassful a day.

A BLOOD PURIFIER can be made from equal parts of Dandelion Root and Leaves (*Taraxacum officinale*), German Camomile Flowers (*Matricaria chamomilla*) and American Senna Leaves (*Cassia marilandica*). Mix well. Steep 2 teaspoonsful in 1/2 cup of boiling water. *Dose:* 1/2 cup morning and evening, made fresh each time.

For CONSTIPATION boil 1 oz. Jalap Root (*Ipomoea jalapa*) and 1 small piece of Aloe (about the size of a pea, says Breac) in 1 pint of water for 10 minutes. Strain and mash the mixture well to get out all possible moisture. *Dose:* 1 wineglassful night and morning.

For DIABETES boil 1 oz. Periwinkle (*Vinca major*) in 1-1/2 pints water for 10 minutes. Allow to cool. *Dose:* 1 wineglassful 3 times a day.

For DIARRHOEA boil 1 oz. of Rhubarb Root in 1 pint of water for 5 minutes. *Dose*: 1/2 wineglassful.

For EYE IRRITATION boil 1 teaspoonful Fennel Seed in 1 pint of water till the water turns golden (don't let it get too dark). Strain and allow to cool. Bathe the eye in the solution 3 times a day.

For HAIR LOSS boil 1 oz. Rosemary (*Rosemarinus officinalis*) in 1 pint of water for 5 minutes. Rub well into scalp on going to bed. Cherry tree bark is also good for this.

For HEADACHES boil 1 oz. Ladies' Slipper Root (*Cypripedium pubesceno*) in 1 pint of water for 10 minutes. Strain and bottle. *Dose:* 1 wineglassful.

For HIGH BLOOD PRESSURE boil 1 oz. of Stinging Nettle (*Urtica dioica*) in 1 pint of water for 5 minutes. Strain then reboil the water before bottling. *Dose:* 1 wineglassful 3 times a day.

For INDIGESTION boil 1 oz. Mandrake Root (*podophyllum peltatum*) in 1 pint of water for 5 minutes. *Dose:* 1 teaspoonful 6 times a day.

For INSOMNIA make a tea of Cowslip Leaves (*Primula veris*). Let it stand for 5 minutes before drinking.

A good LAXATIVE tea can be made as follows: 2 oz. Borage Leaves and Flowers (*Borage officinalis*) mixed with 1 oz. each of Dandelion, Sticklewort (*Agrimonia eupatoria*), and Witch Grass (*Agropyron repens*). Steep 1 tablespoon in 1-1/2 cups of boiling water. *Dose:* 1 tablespoonful, unsweetened.

For MENSTRUAL IRREGULARITIES boil 2 oz. Blue Cohosh Root (*Calilphyllum thalictroides*) in 3 pints of water for 20 minutes. Strain and bottle. *Dose:* 1 wineglassful 2 times a day.

For PILES boil 1 oz. Yellow Dock Root (*Rumex crispus*) in 1-1/2 pints water. Strain. *Dose:* 1 wineglassful morning and night.

For RHEUMATISM boil 1 oz. Dandelion Root in 1-1/2 pints water for 20 minutes. Boil till down to 1 pint of liquid then strain. *Dose:* 1 wineglassful 2 times a day.

A purportedly SEXUAL STIMULANT can be concocted by mixing 1/2 oz. each of False Unicorn (*Helgonias dioica*), Tincture of St. John's Wort (*Hypericum perforatum*) and Tincture of Damiana (*Turnera aphrodisiaca*). *Dose:* 50 drops every 5 hours.

An alternative to the above is to powder and mix equal parts of Damiana Leaves and Saw Palmetta Berries (*Serenoa serrulata*). *Dose:* Take 1 to 2 teaspoonsful a day in water.

The above are good basic recipes for healing a variety

of ills. Learn more. There are plenty of good books on herbs and their uses (see *Bibliography*). Read them.

## EARTH HEALING

There are other ways of healing besides using herbs. One way used a great deal by the PectiWita involves drawing power from the earth and directing it into the patient. This is usually done without the patient being present.

There is a belief held by many people that if we are sick it is for a reason—be it a learning experience or whatever—and therefore nothing should be done to short-circuit that. Others believe that sickness is a sign of the body being "out of balance" and that steps should immediately be taken to bring it back "into balance." There are, of course, many variations on these beliefs. But it should be obvious that it is therefore important that with any form of healing (and any other form of magick, for that matter) there must be *consent* on the part of the recipient. Don't just assume that because someone is sick they will welcome you working to make them well again. Ask them if you may work for them. Get their permission.

Assuming you have that permission, start by preparing as you did in Chapter Seven. Think through carefully what you intend to do and how you intend to do it. Now Ground yourself.

Having Grounded, lay flat upon the ground with your eyes closed, your legs apart and your arms out to the sides at shoulder height—much like a pentagram, or five-pointed star. You can be either face down (sometimes difficult for breathing) or face up, but have the palms of your hands flat on the ground, and your head towards the east.

Now breath deeply and try to sense the energy of the earth. Feel it pulsating; hear the deep, sonorous pulse of

*Earth Healing—drawing power from the earth.*

Nature. Attune yourself to it. Match your breathing to the breathing of the earth. Initially this may sound ridiculous! Give yourself time. You will slowly *sense*—I don't know a better word for this—the beat of life.

Let yourself flow with that beat. Breathe and merge with the ground beneath you. Let yourself become one with the soil or rock on which you lie.

Now ask the earth for healing energy, to be used on another. Think of yourself as a battery. Soak up that energy. Feel it being absorbed into you, through your hands and through your whole body as it presses against the ground. Keep the battery image, so that you don't immediately feel "full." Draw in that energy as an automobile battery does when it is charged; see yourself "on charge."

When you feel you have absorbed all you need—and you will have the capacity to take all you need—turn your mind to the person you wish to heal. See them. Picture them clearly in your mind. See them lying in the same position that you are in. Now, bring the two of you together.

It will be like looking at two images projected onto a screen, side by side. Then the two are moved together to merge and become one. That is how you must see the two of you.

Now feel the energy you have absorbed leaving your body and filling the body of the other person. As you do so, see yourself slowly pulling back; the two images once again separating. But as you are separating you are leaving the healing energy in the other body. Don't hurry this.

Bring yourself back and now see the other person getting to their feet. See them smiling. See them walking; running; jumping; laughing. See them fit and well. Then take your time coming "back" from this. Sit up and relax. Don't dwell on what you've done. Leave the image and the thought of the patient.

The above magickal healing can also be performed using a tree as a conduit to the earth. Rather than lying flat on the ground, sit up against a tree. Face the tree and face east. Wrap both your arms and your legs around the trunk of the tree and continue as above, drawing energy into yourself from the earth, but bringing it up through the tree. Choose a tree where you can wrap yourself around without discomfort. The type of tree is unimportant.

## HANDS-ON HEALING

With the patient present you can do a similar healing, drawing on the power of the earth. Have the patient sit comfortably on the ground, facing east. Stand behind him or her and Ground.

You can either remain standing, or you can kneel, and place your hands on the patient's head or shoulders. Again, as above, attune yourself to the earth. Feel its rhythm and pulse. Draw on its energy. But this time, instead of drawing the energy into yourself, direct it on up through you, down your arms, into the patient. Again, let the "battery" be charged, so do not rush it. And again, as above, finish off by "seeing" the patient standing, running, laughing, etc. When you break contact, give yourself time to recover before standing or moving.

The above two methods of healing are some of the most powerful I have come across in over a quarter century in the Craft. The secret—if secret there be—is not to rush the process. I personally find the absent method preferable to the hands-on.

### HEALING TALISMANS

I talked about talismans and amulets in Chapter Ten. Healing is a common use for these; talismans especially, since they are made for a particular purpose. As in the above mentioned methods of Earth Healing, Healing Talismans are charged through the power of the earth. Stones and wood are therefore popular media for construction.

A light-colored stone should be chosen. It should be as smooth as possible, though whether spherical, oval, or flat is immaterial. Here is one instance where you may go out and search for an appropriate stone, rather than having to use one which just "happens" to come to you. Wash it in a stream and allow it to dry in the heat of the sun.

When you come to do the actual work, work beside a fire, though this does not have to be a large fire. Onto the fire throw some Common Nettle, also Wolf Claw if you can. Ground yourself, then sit comfortably, facing east, the stone on the ground beside you. Close your eyes and place the palms of your hands on the ground to either side. As in the healing work above, attune yourself to the earth. Feel it breathing and pulsating.

When you feel comfortably in tune with the earth, take up the stone and cup it in both hands. Concentrate drawing the earth's healing energies into the stone, allowing them to flow through you and down your arms and hands. Once again, feel that you are charging a battery with this energy.

Relax and place the stone once more on the ground. Bring yourself back and settle yourself. With paint, felt-tipped markers, nail-polish, or whatever, paint the Pictish symbol of Health on the stone. This is a stylized tree (see Chapter Ten). Allow it to dry then hold the stone in the smoke of the natural incense of the fire. Know that the healing energy of the earth is now empowering it. Know that it will serve as a healing stone to whomever may carry it.

If you wish to use wood, rather than stone, cut a piece of wood from a tree. Remember to ask permission of the tree first, explaining the need and purpose. Virtually any wood will do. Oak is good for strength—though a hard wood to carve. Pine is good, for its light color and its ease of carving.

Carve the wood into a size and shape that is pleasing to hold—many choose a flattened rectangle with smoothed edges. Smoothness is probably more important than shape. There is no need to wash the wood in the stream water. Perform the ritual as for the stone, above. You can paint the symbol but I prefer to burn it on, using something that has been heated in the ritual fire.

Wood or stone, the talisman should then be carried by the person needing the healing and placed under the pillow at night. The earth energies will be slowly but surely absorbed as they are needed.

# 14. Survival and Initiation

he PectiWita tradition is one that has lived on, generation after generation, in the Highlands of Scotland. It is a solitary tradition and one especially suited to the rigors of Highland life. Part of that tradition is simply survival.

Today, with so many people living in sprawling cities and towns, talk of survival in the countryside seems a century or more out of step. Yet Aidan Breac never let that side of his teachings die. He was not a doom-sayer or any kind of pessimist; he did not preach the end of the world due to humankind's stupidity (though he certainly mentioned the latter from time to time!). But he was sensible enough to realize that history indicated the wisdom of us having survival skills.

## INITIATION

As you have seen from many of the preceding chapters, much work in this tradition takes place outside, beside streams and on the tops of hills and, in Chapter Three,

I mentioned that there is something akin to the Amerindian vision quest. This is part of the "Initiation," though it is not really a formal Initiation, into the PectiWita. In many, if not most, Wiccan traditions there is a formal coven initiation or a solitary Self Dedication. Not so with the PectiWita. Breac said that the gods know what is in your heart. If you have decided to dedicate yourself to them, to follow the Path of White Light, then there is no need for a formal declaration. Your declaration is in your words and actions, from the present into the future. I can agree with him on that though, as I have stated in other of my books, I do think that a formalization—a "putting into words"—can help the individual set his or her mind to their intent, and to give an official starting point to their path.

If you want to think in terms of a PectiWita initiation ceremony then it must surely be the seven days spent out in the wild, living off the land. During this period you become fully attuned to the earth and learn all about her. You meld with the God and the Goddess and through doing so with all wild life. In learning to recognize what wild plants, roots, fungi, etc., are edible you come to appreciate the completeness of nature; the way in which all things are dependent upon one another, and support one another.

Were you ever in the Boy Scouts or the Girl Scouts? If you were, you probably have already learned some of the basic skills of survival. The military also teaches survival skills, though these are not taught with the correct feeling since it is directed at survival at whatever cost. In the PectiWita training the philosophy is use, not abuse; it is a case of survival through attunement with the rest of nature.

## *SHELTER*

The first thing you need in order to survive in the wild is shelter. Good, light-yet-strong tents are available commercially these days. But, for the moment, forget about commercially produced tents. Let's examine how to make your own temporary tent, and how to make a shelter out of what is to hand. This is the training Breac used to give.

European Gypsies make what they call "Benders." They take long branches of trees—usually hazelnut branches, because they bend easily—stick one end into the ground and then bend them over to stick the other end in. Blankets and/or tarpaulins are spread over a number of these frames and fastened with pieces of wood. Sturdy tents result.

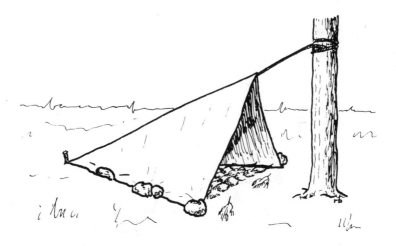

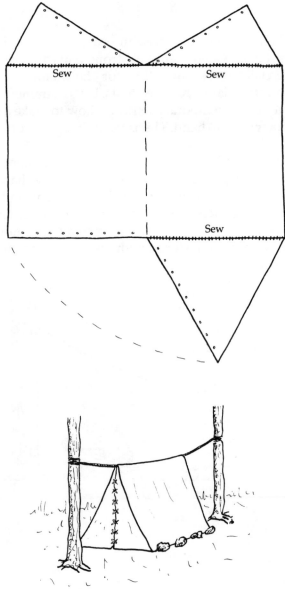

But simple tents can be made with nothing more than a square or rectangle of material, or a poncho. Fasten a line of rope from the branch of one tree to another. Drape the sheeting or poncho over the rope and fasten down or hold down with rocks or earth. If you want to prepare ahead of time, take a sheet of sturdy material approximately ten feet by six feet. Waterproof it by mixing 1/4 pint of copal varnish with 2-1/4 pints of boiled linseed oil. Paint the sheeting with this solution and let it dry in the sun. A second coat can be applied if necessary. A tent dressed with this mixture will withstand the heaviest downpours and it is far superior to commercially produced cans of water-poofing. The ends of such a tent need to be closed, of course. You can do this best by precutting the sheet and sewing it, as shown in the illustration on page 178.

None of Breac's students prepared tents. They made their shelters from what they could find. A favorite was to lean two or three sturdy branches up against a tree, then interweave them and thatch it with smaller sticks and finally leaves, heather, pine branches, and brushwood, to make a natural tent. Do this on the windward side of the tree, so that the opening is in the shelter.

Another way is to make a lean-to in similar fashion. Plant two forked sticks into the ground and run another pole along, resting in the forks. Or simply lay the horizontal pole in the forks of two trees, if there are two appropriately placed. Then lean sticks up against this "ridge pole" and build-up on them. For the final filling-in, with branches of fir trees, reeds, grass, etc., start at the bottom and gradually build up the wall, so that any rain will run off. Again, notice from which direction the wind generally blows and place the back of your shelter that way.

The thicker the roof, the cooler the inside will remain under the sun. If it is too cold at night, cut sod and lay around the base of the wall outside. Don't forget to dig a

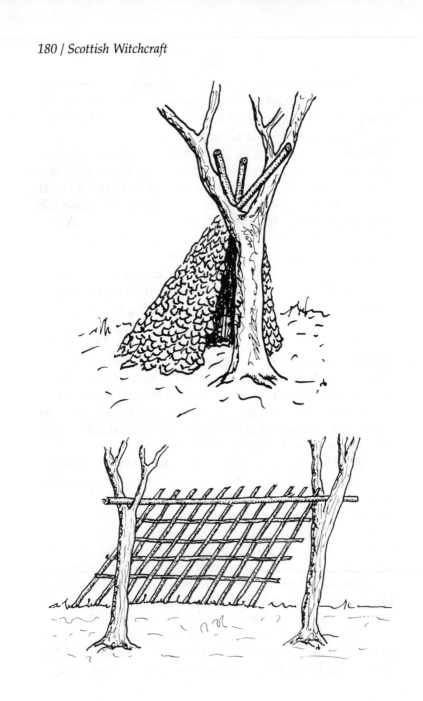

good drain all around your hut/tent, so that if heavy rain comes your floor will not get flooded.

The floor itself is best treated by covering with layers of pine or fir tree branches, straw, bracken, or heather. In fact this makes not only a floor but a fine bed on which to sleep. Remember, the secret to sleeping warmly is to have as much covering underneath you as you have on top. If you cannot get any ground covering for the floor/bed, before lying down make a small hole, about the size of a cup, for your hip joint to rest in when you lie on your side. This can make all the difference to sleeping comfortably.

If there are no poles available, start building up brushwood, heather, small rocks, etc., in a semicircle to at least give you shelter from the wind.

Although there are many bare areas, much of the Highlands has sufficient trees scattered across the hills and mountains that there is no problem making shelters as described above. Similarly in the Eastern United States and other areas. For desert regions, however, there could be a problem. There, the prepared tent, or even the commercial one, is probably your best bet. In some areas of the Highlands where there are few trees, you can find caves in the mountains. These have been utilized by PectiWitans. This may be another possibility for some areas of the United States. In other areas you can build shelter by collecting and piling rocks.

## *HEAT*

You will need a fire, both for warmth and for cooking. You will find that some woods burn better than others. Here is a breakdown of which wood does what:

Apple – burns well with a sweet smell.

Ash – good either green or dry. Easy to chop and split. Lasts longer than most.

Beech – gives a big flame, green or dry.
Birch – lights easily and quickly.
Chestnut – good only when seasoned.
Elder – burns well but the smoke is bitter.
Elm – hard to light. Smoulders with little flame.
Holly – burns well green. Makes good embers.
Lime – gives good heat if dry.
Maple – good heat if dry.
Oak – burns steadily and slowly.
Pine – burns quickly. Good for kindling.
Sycamore – gives good heat but must be dry.

One word of warning for those who live in the Western United States. The shrub Oliander (*Nerium oliander, N. apocynaceae*), and its relative the Yellow Oliander (*Thevetia peruviana, T. neriifolia, T. thevetioides*), are extremely poisonous. Do not use wood for skewers and do not burn the wood. Inhaling the smoke can cause severe irritation of the lungs or worse.

Look for dead wood to make your fire. Apart from not having to cut from the tree, it will also burn more easily. It should be common sense not to start a fire any place where it can easily spread. If there is any dried grass, heather, furze, bracken, or similar, nearby, clear it away. If the ground is covered with grass, clear a circle about three feet in diameter—if necessary digging up sods to leave a bare patch (replacing them when you leave)—and then make your fire in the center. If you can, gather rocks and place around to make a fire circle.

First make a cone of twigs. Those found at the bottom of a hedge are usually very dry and dead and ideal for the purpose. Use those no thicker than a pencil to begin. Build this cone around a wisp of straw, or paper, with a scattering of chips of dead wood on it. Always light your fire from the side the wind is blowing. Add pieces of thicker

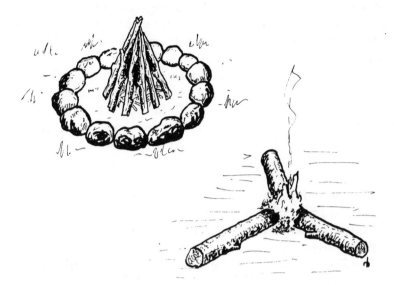

wood as the fire kindles, and so build up on it.

If the weather is wet, look for dead branches and strip the wet bark off them. You will find the wood underneath is dry. Gather your wood early in the day—don't wait till it is dark to do it!

There are three types of material you need for a fire: tinder, kindling, and fuel. *Tinder* is the material that first catches alight. It can be paper, shavings of wood, hay, small dry twigs, dry grass (though dry grass flares very quickly), dry leaves. *Kindling* is a bit bigger than tinder. It can be pieces of wood from the thickness of a pencil up to the thickness of a thumb, and from six to twelve inches long. Large pieces of wood can be split for kindling. This is the wood that is added to the tinder once it catches. It helps the fire gain in strength to the point where it can take the larger fuel and not simply go out. *Fuel* is the real fire material. It can be small or large, though don't try to burn logs that are too huge; split them if need be. It's a good idea to make three piles when gathering wood, dividing into the above categories.

Should you use matches (or a lighter) to start the fire? Obviously you can do what you want. However, as part of the true "getting down to basics" of the PectiWitan sojourn, most Pictish Witches opt to try their hand at starting fire from scratch. It's really not too difficult, with practice. The method favored by Breac involves making a firestarter.

The shaft and the base of the firestarter should be of hardwood (*e.g.* oak). The handpiece can be of either hardwood or of stone. Stone is better, if you can find one with a suitable depression in it, so that the shaft will not slip away as it turns. It should be about three inches in diameter, with a rounded top for comfort in holding it. The shaft should be perfectly straight and round. The bow should be about an inch wide and 1/4 to 5/16 inches thick. The bowstring can be a leather shoelace or strip of rawhide. It is turned once around the shaft.

Place the base of the shaft in the depression in the base and sprinkle some fine straw around it. Press down on the handpiece, and thereby on the shaft. Move the bow back and forth so that it turns the shaft. As it does so, and with the pressure down, the base of the shaft will get extremely hot from friction and will, eventually, set fire to the fine kindling there. From this light some more kindling, if necessary, and from that the fire.

Another method, which I gave in Chapter Nine, is simply to take two sticks, one with a point and the other with a hole in it. The stick with the hole is laid flat on the ground and the other has its point inserted in the hole. The Witan holds the pointed stick between his hands, in an upright position, and twirls the stick, very rapidly.

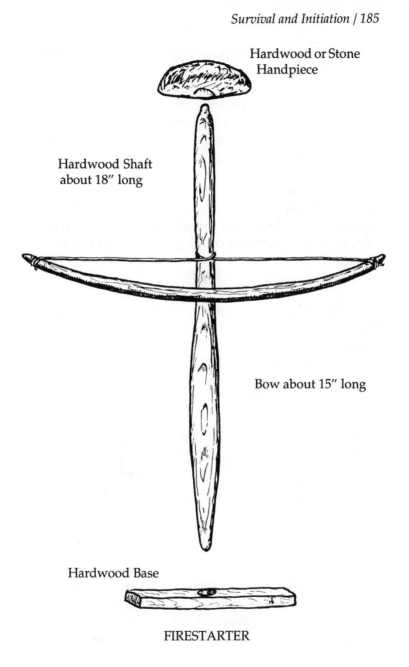

Hardwood or Stone
Handpiece

Hardwood Shaft
about 18″ long

Bow about 15″ long

Hardwood Base

FIRESTARTER

Friction produces a spark, which will ignite any tinder placed around the spinning base.

For a good cooking fire, get a good pile of red hot wood ashes. This can be done by angling three large logs in towards the center, like a three-pointed star. As they burn you keep pushing them in, building up the pile of ashes. This makes a very good cooking fire.

To keep your fire going all night, again make it star shaped and cover it over with a heap of ashes. This will ensure it will keep burning through the night. Practice fire-lighting out of doors. Try it under all conditions: damp, rain, wind. Practice your cooking skills over a campfire.

### COOKING

Pots can be placed on on cooking fires or hung over them. Most utilize pieces of wood and bits of branches found by, or cut from, trees. Here is a wonderful opportunity to be creative!

You should know how to cook meat, fish, and vegetables, and make bread. Meat can be cooked in many ways. It can be stuck through with a stick/skewer and hung over or placed close to the fire. You won't have aluminum foil with you, but you can wrap meat in a few sheets of wet paper, or in a coating of clay, and put in the red hot embers of the fire. Birds and fish can also be cooked this way. There is no need to pluck a bird if you use the clay method. The feathers will stick to the clay as it hardens and come away when you break it open.

Another way to cook a bird is to clean it and then find a stone about the size of its innards. Heat the stone till nearly red hot, place it in the bird, and put the bird on a gridiron or spit over the fire. The stone will cook the inside as the fire cooks the outer part. Remember that birds are more easily plucked immediately after they have been killed.

## HAYBOX COOKING

There is an old Scottish method of cooking that is very economical when you don't have a lot of fuel. It calls for the use of a wooden box filled with hay. It can be very useful since you only have to start the cooking; the haybox finishes it off for you.

Fill a wooden box—about the size of a bread box—with hay (or you can use newspapers or a combination of newspapers and hay). Pack it tightly but leave a space in the center where your cooking pot will fit snugly. Make sure there is plenty of hay below as well as around the pot hole. Make a hay "cushion" to go on the top of the box. Now place your stew, or whatever, on the fire and, as soon as it is well on the boil, take it off and pop it into the hay box, covering it with the cushion of hay. Piling some rocks on top will help hold on the lid and hold in the heat.

Meat will take four or five hours to cook in this way. You can boil oatmeal for five minutes, late at night, and pop it into the box . . . it will be ready for breakfast in the morning.

## BREADMAKING

Favorite with the Picts are bannocks. Make a pile of flour and scoop out the center to form a cup. Pour water into this cup and mix with the flour. Add a pinch of salt and one of baking soda. Knead and mix thoroughly then separate into small rolls of dough. (You will find you need to put some flour on your hands to prevent the dough from sticking to them as you make the bannocks.)

The bannocks can be cooked on a gridiron over the fire but the preferred way is to scrape the fire embers to one side, with a flat piece of wood. The bannocks are then set down on the red hot earth, or stone, and hot ashes are piled all around them. They will then bake themselves.

Another favorite is to cut a long cudgel of wood and to peel and sharpen one end. This end should be heated in the fire. Then make a long strip of dough, about two inches wide and half an inch thick, and wind it spirally down the cudgel. Plant the stick close to the fire, turning it now and again, and it will nicely toast the dough.

## YOUR NATURAL SUPERMARKET

There are an incredible number of plants, herbs, roots, flowers, nuts, berries and fungi that are edible. This applies as much to the United States as it does to Scotland. For meat—without going to large game—there are rabbits, squirrels, various fowls and many varieties of fish. In Appendix B you will find recipes for cooking much of this food so here let us look at gathering, catching and fishing.

## MIND MERGING

One thing Aidan Breac did emphasize, and one which I very much endorse, is that you try to make contact with the animal *or vegetable* beforehand. Ground yourself, then sit or lie on the ground and make contact with the earth, much as you did in Chapter 13. Through the earth, let your mind be led to the vegetation/animal/fish/fowl life you need to acquire. Make mind contact. This can be done much easier if you are within sight of the object, or the home of that object. For instance, on the bank of a stream, the foot of a tree, the edge of a rabbit warren.

Let your mind go out and touch the other form of life. Blend with it. If it is a plant, "feel" the root system spreading out in the earth. Feel the many little root ends stretching out and seeking moisture. Feel the leaves absorbing the light and warmth of the sun. If it is animal, sense the surroundings. Smell the smells; hear the sounds; be aware of the temperatures.

Having blended, start communicating. Introduce yourself as another form of life. Then speak of the balance of nature; how we all live off one another. Explain that you will have need to live off some of that life which you are now contacting. Ask permission that you may join and absorb that life, should it be the will of the gods. State (and mean) that you will only take what you need to survive, and no more.

### RABBITS, HARES AND FISH

Rabbits can be caught fairly easily when driven from their holes. Prepare ahead of time by getting some coarse brown paper and cutting it into strips, about 18 inches long by 2 inches wide. Make up a solution of 1/2 oz Cayenne Pepper, 4 oz Saltpeter, and enough vinegar to mix the two into a paste. Brush this solution over the paper and roll the strips into loose rolls. Allow to dry. When you go rabbiting, place a net over one hole, or set a snare there (see below). Then put one of these rolls into the mouth of the hole on the windward side. Light the roll and, when it is smouldering well, lay a piece of turf over that hole. The rabbit(s) will be driven out into the net or snare.

You can snare rabbits with a noose of copper wire. Take five or six long strands of fine copper wire and twist them together. Or you can strip the plastic covering off electric wire that is composed of several fine strands. Make a slip knot, or sliding noose, in the wire and tie the other end to a stake. The stake can be driven firmly into the ground beside the rabbit hole. The noose is opened just enough to surround the hole entrance. Be sure to wash the wire of all human smell before setting it. When the rabbit runs out of the hole the noose tightens around its neck as it passes through it.

You can tell when there is a rabbit in its hole by the smell—again with a little practice. There is a "warm smell" that comes from an inhabited hole. An uninhabited one smells cold.

Another way to entice rabbits to where you want them, is to make up a mixture of 1/4 oz. Oil of Parsley, 1/2 oz. Oil of Copaiba, 1 dr. Oil of Angelica and 1 dr. Oil of Aniseed. This is actually an old Gypsy trick. Lay a trail from the rabbit hole by putting just a few drops of this mixture on twigs and stones at intervals leading to where you want them.

Hares are relatively easy to catch because they habitually run along the same tracks and always run looking back over their shoulder! They want to see that nothing is following them, presumably. If you find a hare's run you can set a snare somewhere along its length and the hare, running and not looking where it is going, will run into it.

The key to catching fish in the wild is to become familiar with their pattern of life. A fish generally has its own haunt in a stream, feeds at a particular time, and is influenced by weather. Get to know which fish prefer flies and which go for worms. Many can be caught with a small piece of bread for bait.

Trout are fond of sleeping in the shadow of an over-hanging bank. If you lie on your side and very slowly allow your hand to slide into the water where they are, you can—very, very gradually—move your hand to the point where, with fingers curled, you can actually touch the underbellies of the fish. This is known as "tickling" trout. It actually lulls the trout to sleep. Then the secret is to slide the fingers all the way under the fish's belly and quickly flick it up and out of the water onto the bank. This is another Gypsy trick and I have seen my grandfather do it many times.

Perhaps the easiest way to get fish, in small streams, is with a net. Here very small movements and a lot of patience pay off. Don't forget that eels can also be eaten, as can frog's legs. (See Appendix B—*Recipes.*)

You should know how to milk a cow and a goat. A goat is not as easy to milk as might be thought. It has been said that you need to keep hold of its head with one hand, its hind leg with another and then milk it with a third!

## PLANTS, ROOTS AND FUNGI

There are many wild vegetables that you can eat. For example, young stinging nettles (*Urtica dioica*) are as good as spinach, especially when young and tender in the early spring. (They should, of course, be cooked or you'll sting your mouth!) The liquor in which they are boiled is also very good for you, being full of chlorophyll. It's also a great remedy for high blood pressure and hardened arteries. When picking stinging nettles, either wear gloves or grasp them *firmly and solidly* with your bare hands.

The dandelion (*Taraxacum officinale*) is another fine

vegetable. You can boil the leaves or, if young ones, eat them raw in salads. Mix with wild radishes, onions and sorrel leaves (*Rumex acetosa*). The root of the dandelion can give you quite tasty coffee. Dig it up carefully, wash it and dry it. Then roast it over the fire till it is black. Pound it up and you have coffee (also a good liver tonic and good for clearing pimples).

The stems of the common burdock (*Arctium lappa*) may be boiled and eaten. And don't forget watercress (*Nasturtium officinale*), otherwise known as scurvy grass. This grows practically all over the world.

The seeds of crab grass (*digitaria sanguinalis*) are edible. They can be eaten as cereal or ground for flour. Chicory (*Chicorium intybus*) can be eaten raw or cooked like spinach. The roots of the bulrush (*Scirpus* series) can be eaten raw or baked. Yellow Fawn Lilly bulbs (*Erythronium grandiflorum*) can be boiled and eaten.

These days the thing to beware of in gathering your food is pollution. Pass up any edible wild plants growing close to cultivated fields. Fertilizers can give toxic levels of nitrates. Similarly, ignore those close to roadways and exhaust gases. Do not eat any wild plant that you just *think* is edible. Make positive identification.

Along with plants, don't forget barks. For example, the inner bark of the willow tree (*Salix* species), although slightly bitter, is an excellent emergency food. Witans scrape it off, dry it and grind it into flour. The cottonwood (*Populus fremontii*) can be similarly used. The catkins of the cottonwood can also be eaten, either raw or in a stew.

There are literally hundreds of plants, roots, berries, bulbs, nuts, fungi and flowers that are edible. Obviously in one chapter of a book this size it would be impossible to cover them all. You need to acquaint yourself with what is available in your particular area of the world. In the bibliography I list a number of books on this subject. Study them. And let me repeat, make quite sure you have correctly identified a plant before eating it.

## HEIGHT AND DISTANCE

I have already shown you how to determine direction—north, east, south and west (Chapter Nine), for the working of magick. Direction, of course, can also be applied to survival in the wild. In addition to direction, it can help to be able to judge heights and, especially, distances. For example, you might need to fell a tree across a river and therefore need to know the width of the river and be able to find a tree of the right height.

For the height of something, like a tree, pace off from the object eleven paces. Stick a straight branch into the ground at this point . . . you might even be able to use your Staff. Now take one more pace. At this point—twelve paces from the object—put your head down on the ground and sight up at the top of the tree, or object. Reach back and mark on the stick where you see the top. In other words, where your eye, the mark on the stick, and the top of the tree are all in line.

Now measure, on the stick or Staff, the distance in inches from the ground to the mark. Call these inches "feet" and that is the height of the tree. Example: if the mark on the stick is thirty inches up from the ground, the tree is thirty feet tall. Doing this, you can use any unit of measurement—paces, yards, meters—so long as you do eleven and one (twelve in all) and then call the inches on the Staff, feet.

To estimate the distance across a river (or a valley or highway), pick an object on the far side that is at the bank, such as a rock or a tree. Stand directly opposite this object, on your side, and pace out ninety yards along your bank. At the sixty yard point, stick a branch into the ground and then go on the other thirty yards. At that point, turn ninety degrees away from the river and pace out—counting your paces—until, on looking back, the stick is in line with the original object on the far bank. That number of paces is equal to half the width of the river.

There are many other things you could learn that would make survival easier, especially if you had to survive for a longer period than seven days. But I have here covered the basics for you. There are plenty of books available on outdoors life, camping, and survival. Many books on the American Indians also cover this subject. But the best thing is to go out and experience it. It may seem a little frightening at first, but you will quickly settle in. You will probably learn your own special tricks and shortcuts. And you will almost certainly find that it can be a lot of fun.

# 15. City Life and Group Working

hroughout this book I have talked of the PectiWita and its teachings in the same way in which Aidan Breac addressed it. He lived and taught in the Highlands of Scotland. The PectiWita was—and generally is—a religion and practice of the Highlands and the outdoors. I have tried to describe it as such. However, the reality is that more people today live in cities and towns than live out in the country or even within easy access to the countryside. So, just as many people have adopted and adapted Amerindian customs to city life, it will be necessary, and should be quite possible, to do the same with the PectiWita.

Yet I would suggest that no one be too quick to do this. To me, one of the beauties of this tradition of the Craft is its hitherto unspoiled closeness with nature. So much of Wicca—in the short period of time that it has been generally "available" (since the mid nineteen-fifties only)—seems to have lost a lot of its beauty and charm by being adapted to city life. Covens meet in apartment buildings. Electric lights replace candles and oil lamps. A candle in a cauldron has taken the place of the roaring bale-fire. Robes and tools are bought, rather than being handmade by the individual. Ingredients for magick are obtained, ready packaged, from local stores or through mail-order houses.

This is not true of *all* Wiccans, of course. I know there are many who do try to get back to the old ways; who do make the effort to meet outdoors, even when getting there can be an inconvenience. And I think that word "inconvenience" is at the root of all this. Today we hate to be inconvenienced. We are so used to having things prepared for us, of having our lives made easy with labor-saving gadgets, that we have a very low tolerance for any sort of inconvenience.

But there should be a difference between inconvenience and putting effort into something special. To me the Craft is something special—something very special. Looking at the PectiWitan tradition in particular, to me it would be well worth any "inconvenience" to travel out (by car, bus, train, or however) into the great outdoors and to perform the rituals in the way they were originally meant to be performed. To do this would be all part and parcel of honoring the tradition and its rituals.

Having said all that, let's look at the reality of the situation; that fact that (as I said above) more people live in the cities than don't.

Since the PectiWitan tradition is a solitary one it is probably more adaptable than most. Many of its rituals call for the Witan to be high up on a mountain. If you have access to a roof, this could be a step in the right direction. If not, then you will just have to make do in a room in your house or apartment, even if it has to be in the basement! As I mentioned in an earlier chapter, I feel that being outdoors is more important than having the height. If you can get to a city park, or similar, do so. It is often possible to find a quiet spot in one, a little off the beaten track, just enough to do what you need to do. Having a fire, of course, can present a problem. If it is absolutely impossible to have one, then dispense with it. Or you can do as many Wiccan covens do when meeting inside—use a candle to represent the fire. If you do this, then use one of the larger seven-day candles or similar. You can also burn incense in conjunction with the candle/fire. The fire is really all that is called for in the rituals, as a center or focal point.

Unlike other Wiccan traditions, you don't have to worry about setting up an altar and covering it with a large variety of working tools, or with marking out a big circle and setting candles all around it. So, being in a very small apartment need not be a handicap since there is no large circle to cast. All things considered, you could actually perform the PectiWitan rites just sitting on the edge of your bed!

There is call for you to wash certain items in a stream. This can be accomplished by filling a bowl with (bottled) spring water, obtainable from any supermarket. And when it comes to holding any item in the light of the sun or the moon, please take it to an *open* window to do so. Do not have the light coming through glass.

## GROUP WORKING

Some people much prefer to work with others, in a coven situation. I strongly belief that we should all try both arrangements—solitary and coven—before deciding which to stay with. Both have their pros and cons.

It is easy enough to adapt the PectiWitan rites for group working. Mainly it would be the Sabbat rituals that would be involved. For these simply have the leader say the words and the others follow the actions. Or, you could divide up the speaking between several members of the group. Everyone, of course, should do the Centering.

It's as simple as that. None of the rituals is particularly complex so there should be no problems in working them with a number of people. You can, of course (and in fact I recommend that you do), write your own rituals, following the basic feelings of those given.

## CLOTHING

Most Wiccans either go skyclad or wear robes (some few just wear their ordinary, everyday, streetwear). I have long held that you should take a little trouble in preparing yourself for religious ritual. Communing with the Gods is certainly very "special" and, I feel, should be treated as such. I don't think it should be too much to ask Wiccans to dress appropriately. I personally abhor it when a person comes straight into a Circle wearing the same clothes he or she has been wearing all day. It takes but a moment to change, and I think it is downright lazy to glibly give the excuse "The gods know me as I really am." . . . believe me, they do! Let's try to bring a little pride back into the Craft.

So how should you dress for PectiWitan rites? In the Highlands today you see very few Scotsmen wearing the kilt. Some few certainly keep to tradition and do wear it— and wear it proudly—but they seem to be in the minority. I think this unfortunate. I hate to see countries losing their identity, in this world of rapidly increasing uniformity. But many Pictish Witches do wear the kilt for their ritual work. Those who are clan-affiliated, that is.

No, I am not suggesting that everyone interested in Scottish Witchcraft buy a kilt! (They are generally expensive, anyway.) But I do suggest you give some thought to the heritage of this Witan tradition. I have seen some practitioners who have obviously tried to tie-in with the background: some female Witans wearing ankle-length skirts and plain blouses with a tartan sash across one shoulder; males with "Tom Jones" style shirts and pants tucked into boots.

Many actually make their own clothing; some to the point of weaving the cloth for it. If you do this you might also want to use natural dyes. Here is a list of the vegetables used for dyeing, in the old days. They gave wonderful, vibrant colors.

| | |
|---|---|
| Black | Black Alder Bark (*Alnus glutinosa*); Dock Root (*Rumex acetosa; R. crispus*); Blackthorn Bark (*Prunus spinosa*) |
| Grey | Yellow Waterflag Root (*Iris versicolor*); Rowan Bark (*Sorbus aucuparia*) |
| Purple | Sundew (*Drosera rotundifolia*) |
| Violet/Lilac | Black Elder Fruit (*Sambucus nigra*) |
| Blue | Elderberry (*Sambucus nigra*); Woad Leaves (*Isatis tinctoria*); Hollyhock Flowers (*Althaea rosea*) |
| Brown (Dark) | Juniper fruit (*Juniperus communis*) |
| Brown | Dulse (*Rhodymenia palmata*); Iceland Moss (*Centraria islandica*) |
| Brown (Yellowish) | Black Alder Bark (*Alnus glutinosa*) |
| Crimson (Dark) | Dark Lichen |
| Crimson | White Lichen |
| Red | Rue Root (*Ruta graveolens*); Pokeweed Fruit (*Phytolacca americana*) |
| Yellow | Bracken Root (*Pteridium aquilinum*); Bog Myrtle (*Menyanthes trifoliata*); St. John's Wort (*Hypericum perforatum*) |
| Green | Scotch Broom (*Cytisus scoparius*); Coltsfoot (*Tussilago farfara*); Lady's Mantle (*Alchemilla vulgaris*); Larkspur Flowers (*Delphinium consolida*) |

In the final analysis, you must be comfortable in what you wear. As a Solitary tradition, you are the only person who is going to see you, anyway. But, I repeat what I said above—let's try to bring a little pride back into the Craft. Wear something special, that you keep only for your rituals and, if possible, with a tie to the Scottish/Pictish heritage.

## COMMUNICATION WITH THE GODS

The emphasis of PectiWita, as you have seen, is on magickal and divinatory practice rather than on the religion. Yet there are many occasions when the Pictish Witch wants or needs to communicate with the Gods, on a one-to-one basis. This can be done virtually any time and anywhere.

Now may be a good time to think about how, exactly, you picture the God and Goddess. You may associate them with a particular picture or statue you have seen, or a description you have read. Or you may base your idea of them on the feelings you have for and about them. It doesn't really matter how you come upon your particular idea of how they look, so long as that appearance is right for you. It should present the gods in a way in which you can relate to them; a way in which you will always feel comfortable seeing them and talking to them.

Center yourself—again, this can be done anywhere. You could be sitting on a crowded bus or train and simply close your eyes and center yourself. All you really need is to have your feet placed flat on the floor and concentrate on a contact—however circuitous—to the earth. Then do your deep breathing and see and feel the earth colors and energies coming up to fill your body, driving out all negativity, aches, and pains.

Having Centered, now concentrate your thoughts on

the Lord and/or the Lady. See them; see their faces (however you picture them personally). Smile at them. Greet them. Blend with them. Ask what you need to ask and you will receive an answer.

\*      \*      \*

## FINAL WORDS

Although this work has a Pictish background it should be acknowledged that there is, in fact, a synthesis of Pictish, Gaelic and Norse/Saxon cultures contributing to the overall presentation. As Edred Thorsson (*Book of Troth* and *Rune Might*, Llewellyn) was kind enough to point out to me, there is ample evidence of an overriding Scandinavian/Germanic influence, seen especially in some of the terms used here. Edred said, "The Scottish dialect of English is full of Scandinavian words due to the prolonged and ancient influence of that culture upon that country and the northern half of England." A fact of which Aidan Breac may or may not have been aware.

Aidan Breac's training consisted mainly of developing a true feeling for the Craft in the individual Witch. The PectiWitan was encouraged to work on establishing a clear mental picture of the Witan way of life and of the Gods. This alone could take days, weeks, or even months. Reading any and all available books on Witchcraft and allied subjects is important . . . read and have an opinion on what you have read. Attunement with the rest of nature is of paramount importance.

Training for the seven day Survival/Initiation was long and detailed with Breac. Following it, a thorough recapitulation of the seven days would be gone over by the

Student and Master together, to find what had been learned. This is certainly something you can do alone—review your seven days and examine your experiences minutely. What did you learn? How did this bring you into contact with Mother Earth and the life upon/within it? Has this changed, or reconfirmed, your feelings and empathy with this life?

No book can take the place of the personal one-on-one teaching that was given. I have tried to touch (however briefly) upon all that Breac taught, but this is but a small sampling. However, you should be able to take what I have given you and work on it, and on yourself, to the point where you could be a Witan that Breac would be proud of. I hope you will do so.

Raymond Buckland

# Appendix A
## PectiWitan Runes and Pictish Glyphs

In making talismans the PectiWita frequently use the elaborate Pictish Glyphs or the PectiWitan Runes. Also, occasionally, the *Ogham Bethluisnion*, alphabet. I presented these (the Pictish Glyphs and the PectiWitan Runes for the first time ever in print) in my book *Buckland's Complete Book of Witchcraft*. I reprint them here, since they pertain specifically to Scottish Witchcraft.

### OGAM BETHLUISNION

The early Kelts and their priests, the Druids, had their own form of alphabet. It was known as *Ogam Bethluisnion*. It was an extremely simple form and was used more for carving into wood and stone than for general writing. With a center line, it lent itself especially to carving along the edge of a stone or a piece of wood.

| b | l | f | s | n | h | d | t | c | q | ea | ia |
|---|---|---|---|---|---|---|---|---|---|----|----|

æ   m   g   ng   st   r   a   o   u   e   i

## PICTISH

The PectiWita have two interesting forms of magickal writing. One is a variation on runes and the other is based on the old and very decorative Pictish script. As with other runes, the Pictish ones are made up entirely of straight lines. The way they are put together, however, requires some study. Basically they are used with *phonetic* spelling. That means, spelling a word the way it sounds. The English language has a ridiculous number of words spelled nothing like the way they are pronounced. For example, *bough* (the limb of a tree), *cough, through, though, thought*... all have the *ough* spelling, yet all are pronounced differently! Spelling those words phonetically they would be: *bow, coff, throo* or *thru, thoe* and *thot*. This is the basis of PectiWita runes; things are spelled as they are pronounced. Now with the examples just given, *through* could be either *throo* or *thru*, so let's look at the pronunciation of vowel sounds. "A" can be *a* as in *hat*, or *ā* as in *hate*. "E" can be *e* as in *let* or *ē* as in *sleep*. "I" can be *i* as in *lit* or *ī* as in *light*. "O" can be *o* as in *dot* or *ō* as in *vote*. "U" can be *u* as in *cup* or *ū* as in *lute*. By putting the bar over the letter (ā, ē, ī, ō, ū) we can indicate the hard sound and so differentiate from the soft sound. This is how it is indicated in the Pictish runes:

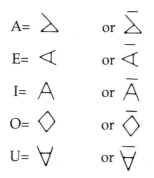

We can go a step further with these runes. Vowels are pronounced differently when put with an "R" (ar, er, ir, etc.) or with another vowel and "R" (air, ear, ere, our, etc.). To indicate these, then, the symbol ∧ is used over the vowel.

△̂ = ar, ae, air;

◁̂ = er, ere, ear, eir;

Â = ir, ire;

◇̂ = or, ore, our, ow;

∀̂ = ur, ure.

If this sounds complicated, bear with me. You will find that, with a little practice, it is really quite easy. [A point to remember if you just *can't* get it no matter how hard you try, then just go ahead and spell out the words substituting rune for letter without regard for phonetics. But do give it a good try first, please.]

A final note on the vowels. As in Hebrew, the vowel is written *above* the line, in Pictish runes, rather than with

the consonants. Much like this: Th<sup>e</sup> v<sup>o</sup>w<sup>e</sup>l <sup>i</sup>s wr<sup>i</sup>tt<sup>e</sup>n
<sup>a</sup>b<sup>o</sup>v<sup>e</sup> th<sup>e</sup> l<sup>i</sup>n<sup>e</sup>. (Phonetically this would be: Th<sup>e</sup> v<sup>ô</sup>el is
r<sup>i</sup>t<sup>e</sup>n <sup>a</sup>b<sup>u</sup>v th<sup>e</sup> l<sup>i</sup>n.)

Here are the complete PectiWita Runes:

You will notice that there is no "C," "Q" or "X". The
reason is the use of the phonetic spelling. In the English
language "C" is either pronounced the same as an "S" (as
in *cease*) or the same as "K" (as in *escape*), so there is really
no need for the "C." Similarly, "Q" is pronounced "kw"

(*e.g.* quick = kwik) and "X" is pronounced "eks" (*e.g.* eksaktli), so they are unnecessary. Single runes are given for "ch," "sh," "th," "gh" and "ng." Here are one or two examples of phonetic spellings using these:

THING — ⟨runes⟩

TAUGHT — ⟨runes⟩

CHOOSE — ⟨runes⟩

QUICKLY — ⟨runes⟩

COME — ⟨runes⟩

Hopefully you can see that this is really not too difficult and can actually be a lot of fun. A few more examples might help:

"THESE ARE EXAMPLES OF HOW

| | | | | | |
|---|---|---|---|---|---|
| *Phonetically:* | Thēs | ar | eksampls | of | how |
| *PectiWita Runes:* | ⟨runes⟩ | | ⟨runes⟩ | ⟨runes⟩ | ⟨runes⟩ |

THE PECTIWITA RUNES ARE

| | | | |
|---|---|---|---|
| *Phonetically:* | thē | Pekti-Wita | rūns | ar |
| *PectiWita Runes:* | ⟨runes⟩ | ⟨runes⟩ | ⟨runes⟩ | ⟨runes⟩ |

USED. AS YOU CAN SEE, THEY CAN

*Phonetically:* ūsd. As ū kan sē, thā kan

*PectiWita Runes:*

ACTUALLY LOOK VERY

*Phonetically:* aktūali luk veri

*PectiWita Runes:*

ATTRACTIVE."

*Phonetically:* atraktif.

*PectiWita Runes:*

Some PectiWitans go just one step further by running all the words together and using a "+" to indicate separations:

etc.

*Warning:* DO NOT TRY TO SLANT YOUR RUNES (these or any other ones); KEEP THEM UPRIGHT.

The Picts were better known for their elaborate "swirl" style of writing. This is much more straightforward than the above runes in that it is not done phonetically, and the vowels are kept on a level with the consonants. It is simply a matter of substituting the Pictish symbol for the letter. The symbols are rather elaborate, however, and you need to be careful in doing them to avoid confusion. Again single symbols are included for "ch," "sh," "th," "gh," and "ng."

| | | |
|---|---|---|
| A – ⊚ | K – 𝄢 | U – 𝄞 |
| B – 𝄢 | L – 𝄢 | V – 𝄢 |
| C – 𝄢 | M – 𝄢 | W – 𝄞 |
| D – 𝄢 | N – 𝄢 | X – 𝄢 |
| E – 𝄢 | O – ⊚ | Y – 𝄢 |
| F – 𝄢 | P – 𝄢 | Z – 𝄢 |
| G – 𝄢 | Q – 𝄢 | CH – 𝄢 |
| H – 𝄢 | R – 𝄢 | SH – 𝄢 |
| I – 𝄢 | S – 𝄢 | TH – 𝄢 |
| J – 𝄢 | T – 𝄢 | GH – 𝄢 |
| | | NG – 𝄢 |

Here are a few examples of using the pictish script:

"T H E     P I C T S     W E R E

V E R Y     C L E V E R     I N

T H E     U S E     O F

O R N A M E N T A L D E S I G N.

P I C T I S H   A R T W O R K   W A S

L A T E R   A D O P T E D   B Y   T H E

K E L T S,   E S P E C I A L L Y   T H E

I R I S H   K E L T S."

# Appendix B
# Recipes

The Scots have some great recipes unique to their corner of the globe. I could fill a whole book with them, but I am going to stick with those that would be most useful to you on your seven day sojourn into the mountains. Here are a few; some are Breac's favorites and some are taken from my grandmother's Gypsy recipe book. All can be cooked on top of a fire; none call for an oven.

CROWDIE

A Scottish standby. There are several kinds of Crowdie (one is actually a form of cheese), but this is the basic one favored by most "survivalist" PectiWitans. There is really no "recipe" as such, since it is simply coarse oatmeal stirred together with some milk (or water). It can be heated but is more usually served cold. The Highland name is actually *Fuarag*, but it is certainly better known as Crowdie, the Lowland name for it.

PORRIDGE (*Brochan*)

Use good oatmeal, not too finely ground. Bring water to a boil and then "trickle" the oatmeal into it, stirring with a spurtle (wooden stick) as you do so. Let the porridge cook for about a half-hour. Keep stirring, keeping an eye out for lumps. When the porridge is half done—and not before—add a pinch of salt.

Some say that when the porridge is boiling steadily you should pull the pot off the fire, cover it with a tight lid, and allow it to stand for twenty minutes or so.

Traditionally porridge is eaten while standing, and is referred to as "them." It can be eaten with milk or butter-milk, and with salt. It should never be sweetened. In *The Scots Kitchen*, F. Marian McNeill suggests to allow one breakfastcupful of water, one handful of oatmeal and a small teaspoon of salt, for each person.

## DRAMMACH

This is a beverage which McNeill describes as "the hiker's special." Oatmeal, seasoned with salt and pepper, is mixed with cold water until thin enough to drink. Robert Louis Stevenson said that this not only quenches the thirst but "provides a good enough dish for a hungry man, and where there are no means of making fire, or good reasons for not making one, it is the chief stand-by of those who have taken to the heather."

## BLOATERS

These are fat herrings or mackerels, lightly salted and smoked, that are very popular in Britain. There is a knack to cooking them well. First open the bloaters by slitting their bellies. Cut off the heads and take out the insides. (They will now look very much like kippers.) Put a piece of butter on the inside fleshy part and lay the fish in the frying pan, skin side down. Then place a second bloater on top of the first, sandwich fashion, skin side up. Fry the bot-tom fish for a couple of minutes, then turn the top one down and give it the same treatment. Only the *skin* sides of the fish should touch the pan. Served with salt and pepper to taste, they are delicious!

## FRIED HERRINGS

Split, bone, clean and dry the herrings. Sprinkle them with salt and pepper, then roll them in oatmeal. Put some dripping in the frying pan and heat it. When it smokes blue, put the fish in. Fry until they are well browned on both sides.

## EELS

From my Gypsy recipe book. To cook eels, skin them and wash them, then cut them up and place in a pan of slightly salted water. Add some finely chopped parsley. Boil the eels until they begin to break open slightly. Stir in a little flour to thicken the liquid. Serve the eels hot with boiled potatoes.

## RABBIT

Here are a few rabbit recipes. Again, from my Gypsy recipe book.

## RABBIT STEW (i)

Skin the rabbit and clean it. Cut off the legs and divide the body section into three parts and place in the pan with water. Add an onion or two (Gypsies sometimes add pickled belly of pork, for extra taste), and boil for one and a quarter hours. Then add a few potatoes and boil for another half hour.

## RABBIT STEW (ii)

Cut the meat into small pieces, roll in seasoned flour and brown. Make sure every piece is well browned for best flavor. Add two cups of water and simmer in tightly covered pan till meat is tender (about one and a half hours). Add vegetables cut into fairly large chunks (potatoes, carrots, onions) and continue cooking in covered pan until vegetables are tender. Add a little flour to thicken broth if desired (mix flour with cold water first). Serve steaming hot.

### FRIED RABBIT

Cut the rabbit up into pieces and roll in a mixture of one cup of flour, one teaspoon of salt, and pepper to taste. Brown the rabbit in at least four tablespoons of cooking fat. Add one diced onion and a little lemon juice, if you have it. Cover and cook till done.

### CREAMED SOUR RABBIT

Cut the rabbit into small pieces and soak it overnight in one cup of vinegar and half a cup of water. Next morning, cook the rabbit in the vinegar solution until done, thickening the broth with a little flour. Salt and pepper to taste and serve hot.

### FRIED QUAIL

Pluck and clean the quail. Cut it up into pieces—breast and two legs is good. Season with salt and pepper and roll the pieces in flour. Place in hot deep fat and brown quickly on both sides. Cover the pan and lower the heat. Let it cook slowly till tender. You can make a gravy in the same pan, mixing flour in with the residue left over from frying.

### FROG LEGS

Skin the frog legs, wash them and cut off the feet. Soak at least an hour in salt water, then season with salt and pepper. Lightly beat an egg. Dip the legs in breadcrumbs, then in the egg, and again in the breadcrumbs. Fry in deep hot fat.

BURN TROUT

The trout should be slightly salted and then left to lie overnight. Next morning wipe them, sprinkle with salt and pepper, dip in milk and roll in coarse oatmeal. Cook very quickly in smoking hot lard, browning both sides.

PIGTAIL POTATOES

Peel some potatoes then, with a sharp knife (or parer), cut in long, thin strips. Soak the strips in cold water for at least an hour then carefully dry. Fry in deep hot fat.

POACHERS' STEW

Another from my Gypsy recipe book. This is good for rabbit, squirrel, hedgehog, coon, possum, ground hog, turtle—just about any kind of meat you can catch or trap.

Cut meat into small chunks and season with salt and pepper. Peel and dice an onion then brown the meat and onion in a pan with fat. When well browned, pour off any excess fat. Add two cups of water, cover the pan and simmer for one and a half to two hours or till meat is tender.

Cut up potatoes, carrots, turnips, parsnips, and any other vegetables, and toss into the pot. Keep the lid on and simmer till vegetables are tender.

OATMEAL SOUP

Melt some butter in a large pan over a low heat. Add chopped onions and grated carrot and cook gently for about six minutes. Add two ounces of oats and continue cooking for about four minutes, stirring frequently. Add about a pint of chicken stock, little by little, bring to the boil and simmer, covered, for about thirty minutes. Add some parsley, a pint of milk or water, and heat through, though do not bring to the boil.

SKIRLIE

Melt a little butter or dripping over a medium heat

and add a finely chopped onion. Stir until the onion is browned. Add oatmeal, slowly, until all the fat is absorbed and the mixture is fairly firm. Add seasoning and keep stirring for about eight minutes.

Skirlie is very good with fish.

### STOVIE TATTIES

Cut up two or three onions into small pieces and fry them together with small scraps of meat. Peel and cut up into small pieces about a half-dozen large potatoes. Put the pieces of potato into a pan with sufficient water to cover the bottom. Add small pieces of butter. When the butter has melted and run through the potato, add the fried meat and onions. Salt and simmer slowly, covered, until the potatoes are quite soft.

### HEATHER ALE

If you need something to wash down all this good food, you might make some Heather Ale ahead of time, and take with you. Scottish folklore has it that the original brewers of Heather Ale were the Picts—and they brewed the finest ale imaginable! The Scots tried to discover the secret, which was known only to the Pictish King and his son, but both died rather than tell. So the Heather Ale brewed by the Scots today is a far cry from the wonderful stuff brewed originally by the Picts!

When the heather is in full bloom, gather heather-bells and wash them thoroughly in cold water. Fill a pot with the heather-bells and cover with water. Boil for an hour then strain the liquid into a clean wooden tub. For every dozen pints, add half an ounce of hops, an ounce of ground ginger, and a pound of sweet treacle or honey. Boil again for another twenty minutes then strain off once more. When almost cold, add five tablespoonsful of barm (brewer's yeast). Cover with a cloth and allow to work undisturbed for at least twenty-four hours. Skim carefully, and pour gently into a tub, leaving all the barmy sediment behind. Put into bottles and cork tightly. Store in a dark place for at least a week.

## PIRR

A recipe for a beverage, from the Shetlands. Mix two tablespoonsful of oatmeal with a teaspoonful of sugar and a quarter teaspoonful of Cream of Tartar in a warm jug. Add just enough cold milk to make a smooth paste. Then pour in half a pint of boiling water, stirring all the time. Allow to cool, or can be drunk hot.

## BLAAND

Also from the Shetlands, this drink is simply the whey of buttermilk left to ferment in an oak cask. To make the whey, pour enough hot water on the buttermilk to cause it to separate. Drain the whey off the curd (which may be pressed and eaten with cream). Pour the whey into the cask and leave undisturbed until it reaches the fermenting, sparkling stage, when it may be used.

After the sparkle goes off it, Blaand becomes flat and vinegary but you can keep it at its best stage by the regular addition of fresh whey.

## HAGGIS

Haggis is not the sort of thing you would be likely to try to cook on a survival trip, but I couldn't resist including a recipe for it since it is probably the best known of Scottish dishes. The following is, in fact, regarded by some as "the" recipe—the one with which Meg Dods won the great Competition of Haggises in Edinburgh, in the beginning of the nineteenth century, "when the Cleikum Haggis carried the stakes and that of Christopher North came in second"! Try it at home. It is really quite delicious.

You need a sheep's pluck (this includes heart, lights, and liver) and paunch, onions, oatmeal, beef-suet, pepper, salt, cayenne, vinegar or lemon.

"Clean a sheep's pluck thoroughly. Make incisions in the heart and liver to allow the blood to flow out, and par-boil the whole, letting the windpipe lie over the side of the pot to permit the discharge of impurities; the water may be changed after a few minute's boiling. A half hour's boiling will be sufficient; but throw back the half of the liver to boil till it will grate easily; take the heart, the half of the liver, and part of the lights, trimming away all skins and black-looking parts, and mince them together. Mince also a pound of good beef-suet and four or more onions. Grate the other half of the liver. Have a dozen of small onions peeled and scalded in two waters to mix with this mince. Have ready some finely ground oatmeal, toasted slowly before the fire for hours, till it is of a light-brown colour and perfectly dry. Less than two teacupsful of meal will do for this quantity of meat. Spread the mince on a board and strew the meal lightly over it, with a high seasoning of pepper, salt, and a little cayenne, first well mixed. Have a haggis bag (*i.e.* a sheep's paunch) perfectly clean, and see that there be no thin part in it, else your whole labour will be lost by its bursting.

"Some cooks use two bags, one as an outer case. Put in the meat with a half-pint of good beef gravy, or as much strong broth as will make it a very thick stew. Be careful not to fill the bag too full, but allow the meat room to swell; add the juice of a lemon or a little good vinegar; press out the air and sew up the bag, prick it with a large needle when it first swells in the pot to prevent bursting; let it boil slowly for three hours if large."

My wife has made excellent haggis using a plastic baking bag, rather than a sheep's stomach, and getting the heart and liver separately.

# Appendix C
## Witchcraft . . . The Religion

*The small booklet* Witchcraft . . . the Religion, *was first published in 1966 by The Buckland Museum of Witchcraft and Magick, in New York. It was published as a primer on Wicca; the sort of thing that one could pass out to friends who might express interest and/or curiosity on the subject. I reproduce the first part of it here as a supplement to the earlier chapters of this book, on the history of Witchcraft.*

### WITCHCRAFT . . . THE RELIGION
### by Raymond Buckland
*Copyright © 1966 Raymond Buckland*

Witchcraft is a religion. This simple statement comes as a surprise to many people, yet it is a fact; Witchcraft is a religion. Furthermore, it is one of the oldest religions, if not the oldest, known to man.

The God of Witchcraft first appeared in Paleolithic times as the God of Hunting. As such he was naturally depicted as being horned, like the animals hunted. In those days in order to survive man had to have success in the hunt. There had to be food to eat, skins for warmth and shelter, bones to fashion into tools and weapons. One of the earliest illustrations of a priest representing this God is to be found in the *Caverne des Trois Frères*, Ariége, and known as *The Sorcerer*. This shows a man dressed in the skin of a stag and wearing a mask and horns. He is performing some sort of ritual to ensure success in the hunt. In Dordogne is found another, lesser known, cave painting of a man again dressed in a skin, this time wearing the mask and horns of a bull. He is playing some form of musical instrument while, again, leading a ritual.

It is interesting to see how this form of sympathetic magick, to ensure success in the hunt, has survived right through to the present day. The American Penobscot Indians, for example, wear a deer mask and horns when performing a ritual for the same purpose. The Mandan Indians' Buffalo Dance is another excellent example.

Magick played an important part in the life of Neanderthal Man, as it does today in the lives of many people throughout the world. Two interesting forms of this sympathetic magick are to be found in the Ariége caves. Sympathetic magick is the belief that like attracts like. The most common example of this type of magick is the "waxen image," which has been used for thousands of years. It was a means of working evil against one's enemies. A model of the enemy was made in clay, or beeswax, or some similar substance. While making it, however crude the likeness in itself, the operator had to have a clear picture of the victim in his mind all the time. If something belonging to the intended victim could be mixed in with the wax, all the better. Preferable were actual parts such as nail-parings or locks of hair. Some of the extant examples of these figures are beautifully made; every feature worked in. Others are crude, simple little "gingerbread" forms. When made the figures would be given the victim's name and then either stuck with pins or slowly melted over a flame. As the figure slowly melted, so would the actual person sicken and waste away. In the case of the pins he would feel sharp pains until, finally, a pin through the heart would finish him! This was supposed to be a most potent form of magick.

The Ancient Egyptians were known to have used it. It is also to be found with the American Indian—the Modoc tribe, for example—the Australian aboriginal, and in many countries around the world. The Berwick Witches in their plot with Francis, Earl Bothwell, against King James VI, was a famous example of the "making of a waxen image."

The examples of sympathetic magick at *Le Tuc d'Audoubert*, Ariége, are probably the oldest. The first is a large, clay model of a bison—very realistic—on the floor of the cave. This model is pock-marked with dozens of holes where it was literally attacked with spears, javelins and arrows, by the Neanderthal hunters acting out the hunt before going out to the real thing.

The second example is of sympathetic magick being used this time not to injure but to bring about fertility. It is another large, clay model, this time of a male bison mounting a female. Fertility amongst the animals was as important, at this time, as fertility amongst the people. There had to be sufficient numbers of animals to be hunted for food, clothing, etc., and there had to be sufficient children in the tribe to survive the many perils of the age and carry on the tribe's existence.

Although the first cave paintings representing a deity were of the Horned God, the first carvings were of a Mother Goddess. There are a number of early examples of these carvings in existence, known generally as Venus figurines. The Willendorf Venus is perhaps one of the best known; another similar one being the Venus of Sireuil.

The Venus of Laussel is another fine example, though it is not a complete figure in itself, being carved in relief in the rock wall of the cave. It is probably impossible to say which came first, the god or the goddess representations, if in fact either one did come before the other. It seems far more likely that they both came into being at the same time.

The Mother Goddess figures have several things in common. The main points being the emphasis of the feminine attributes—heavy, pendulous breasts, big buttocks, pregnant-like belly, exaggerated sex organs—and the complete lack of identity with the face. In many examples the arms and legs are either non-existent or at least barely suggested. The reason for this style was that humankind was only concerned with the fertility aspect. Woman was the bearer and nurser of the young; the Goddess was her representative as the Great Provider and Comforter: Mother Nature or Mother Earth.

At a later stage, when agriculture was introduced and established, the Goddess came more to the fore. When humankind had relied exclusively on hunting it was the God who was the more important but later, with her fertility aspect—for crops as well as for man and beast—it was the Goddess. This relationship has stayed in Witchcraft right through to the present day. Of the two main deities, the Goddess, in many traditions, is regarded as being more important than the God.

As humankind developed so did religion—for that is what it had become. It developed slowly and naturally. Man spread across Europe taking the gods with him. In different countries the gods would perhaps be known by different names, but they were essentially the same gods. The Horned God, originally of hunting, now looked upon more as the God of Death and what came after; and the Goddess, of Fertility and Rebirth. Not only would the gods have different names in different countries, but the same was true in different areas of one country. A good example is to be found in England where, in the south, is found the god *Cernunnos* ("The Horned One"). A little further north is found the same horned god, this time known as *Cerne*. In another area still the name has become *Herne*.

It has been shown that the "Old Religion" was a natural one, developing gradually and easily as humankind developed. It was basically a very simple, uncomplicated religion, as can be seen from Witchcraft as it is today. The priests and priestesses of the Old Religion were known as the *Wica* (or *Wicca*), an Anglo-Saxon word meaning "the Wise Ones." It is from this word *wica* that the word "witch" is derived. These people really were the Wise Ones. They invariably had a great knowledge of herbs and acted as doctor as much as priest. They would lead the simple rituals, know all the magicks, and on the Great Festivals would be, to the people, the living embodiment of the God and Goddess.

With the coming of Christianity there was *not* the immediate mass conversion that is often suggested. Christianity was a "man-made" religion as opposed to the natural, gradual development we have seen with the Old Religion. Whole countries were classed as Christian when it was only the rulers who had, often superficially, adopted the new religion. In Europe generally the Old Religion was still in prominence for the first thousand years of Christianity. It is still alive today and beginning to grow again as people, thinking for themselves, find how much more attractive it is than the artificiality of the general forms of monotheism.

When the first Christian churches were being built, the only craftsmen available—stone-masons; wood-carvers—were Pagans. When these artisans were made to build the churches they very cleverly put figures representing their own gods in with the other, often ornate, decorations in wood and stone. Many of these figures can still be seen today, on old English churches. The Goddess fertility figure was usually depicted with her legs spread wide, displaying greatly enlarged genitalia. The God was shown as a God of Nature, with his horned head surrounded by—or even entirely composed of—foliage, fruit, etc. For this reason these old carvings of the God are called "Foliate Masks," or "Jack of the Green," or "Robin o' the Woods." It is a motif which has retained its popularity right through to the present day. Comparatively modern buildings are often decorated with various forms of the old pagan foliate mask—though it is doubtful if many of the architects are aware of its derivation!

If the old Pagan artisans were clever in putting their old gods in the new churches, the early Christians were equally clever in their choice of sites for these churches. The orders of Pope Gregory to his priests in England contained a section telling them that, whenever possible, they should build their churches on the sites of the Pagan temples and meeting places, so that people would, out of habit, continue to come there.

In those days, when Christianity was slowly growing in strength, the old Pagan religion was its rival. It is only natural to want to get rid of a rival and the Church pulled no punches to do just that. The god of the Pagans had horns. So, apparently, had the Christians' Devil. Obviously then, reasoned the Church, the Pagans were Devil-worshippers! This type of reasoning is used by the Church even today. Missionaries were particularly prone to label all primitive tribes, upon which they happened to stumble, as "Devil worshippers," just because the tribe worshipped a god or gods other than the Christian one. It did not matter that the people were good, happy, often morally and ethically better living than the vast majority of Christians—they had to be converted!

The charge of Devil worship, so often leveled at Witches, is ridiculous. The Devil is a purely Christian invention; there being no mention of him, as such, before the New Testament.* Since the Old Religion stems from long before the start of Christianity obviously Witches do not even believe in the Devil, let alone worship him!

As Christianity gradually grew in strength so the Old Religion was slowly pushed back. Back until, about the time of the Reformation, it only existed in the outlying country districts. The word "pagan" comes from the Latin *pagani*, meaning "people who live in the country." Similarly, the word "heathen" simply means "people who live on the heath." Since this now inferred people following the Old Religion such followers were dubbed "Pagans" and "Heathens." The words are often used today in a derogatory sense, which is incorrect.

As the centuries passed the "smear campaign" against the Wica intensified. Everything they did was reversed and used against them. They did magick to promote fertility and increase the crops; the Church therefore claimed that they made women and cattle barren and blighted the crops! No one, apparently, stopped to think that if the Witches really did that they would suffer equally themselves, since they too had to eat to live! An old act of fertility was for the villagers to go to the fields, in the light of the full moon, and dance around the field astride pitchforks, poles, broomsticks, etc., riding them like hobby-horses. They would leap high in the air to show the crops how high to grow. A harmless enough

---

* It is interesting to note that the whole concept of Evil associated with the Devil is due to an error in translation, the original Old Testament Hebrew *Ha-satan* and the New Testament Greek *diabolos* simply meaning "opponent" or "adversary."

form of sympathetic magick. But no! The Church claimed not only that they were working against the crops but that they were actually flying through the air on their pitchforks and broomsticks! Surely an act of the Devil!

In 1484 Pope Innocent VIII produced his Bull against Witches, and two years later two infamous German monks, Heinrich Institoris Kramer and Jakob Sprenger, produced their incredible concoction of anti-witchery, the *Malleus Malleficarum* ("The Witches' Hammer"). Definite instructions were given, in the book, for the prosecution of Witches. When, however, the book was submitted to the Theological Faculty of the University of Cologne—the appointed censor of books at that time—the majority of the professors refused to have anything to do with it. The office of censoring books was shortly removed from the university by papal order and given to the bishops, while Kramer and Sprenger, nothing daunted, forged the approbation of the whole faculty. This forgery was exposed in 1898, by the Cologne archivist.

Gradually the hysteria kindled by Kramer and Sprenger began to spread. It spread like a fire—flashing up suddenly in unexpected spots; spreading quickly across the whole of Europe. For nearly three hundred years the fires of the persecution raged. Mankind had gone mad! In 1586 the Archbishop of Treves "discovered" that the local Witches had "caused" the severe winter of 1585! By dint of frequent torture a "confession" was obtained and one hundred twenty men, women and children were burned on his charge that they interfered with the elements! The inhabitants of entire villages where one or two Witches were suspected of living would be killed with the cry "Destroy them all! The Lord will know His own!"

A rough estimate of the total number of people—men, women and children—burned, hung, or tortured to death, on the charge of Witchcraft, is NINE MILLION. Obviously not all of these were really followers of the Old Religion. In fact, many were devout Christians! But this had been a wonderful opportunity to "get rid of" *anyone* against whom one bore a grudge. Just to murmur "Witch!" was enough.

An excellent example of the way in which the hysteria developed and spread is the case of the so-called "Witches" of Salem, Massachusetts. It is doubtful if any of the victims hung* there were really followers of the Old Religion. (Just possibly Bridget Bishop and Sarah Good, but of the others, they were nearly all pillars of the local church up until the time the hysterical children "cried out" upon them.) The whole case is dealt with extremely well by Marion L. Starkey in her book *The Devil In Massachusetts*.

In 1604 King James I passed his Witchcraft Act but this was repealed in 1736. It was replaced by an Act which stated that there was no such thing as Witchcraft and to pretend to have occult powers was to face being charged with fraud!

By the late seventeenth century the surviving members of the Wica had gone underground. Christianity had shown its new strength in no uncertain terms—those it could not convert it would destroy! For the next three hundred years to all appearances Witchcraft was dead. But a religion which had lasted twenty thousand years or more did not die so easily. In small groups—surviving covens, oftimes consisting only of family members—the Craft continued.

In the literary field Christianity had a heyday. Until the early part of the twentieth century everything written

---

* In New England the law was as in England; Witches were hung, not burned. In Scotland and in Continental Europe burning was the penalty.

about Witchcraft was written from the Church point of view. It was not until Dr. Margaret A. Murray, in 1921, produced *The Witch Cult In Western Europe* that anyone looked at Witchcraft with anything like an unbiased light. From studying the records of the trials of the Middle Ages, Dr. Murray, an eminent folklorist and Professor of Egyptology at London University, picked up the clues that showed there was a definite organized, pre-Christian religion behind all the hogwash of the Christian allegations. She enlarged on this in her book *God Of the Witches* (1931) and actually traced the cult back to its Paleolithic origins.

In 1954 Dr. Gerald B. Gardner, in his book *Witchcraft Today*\* said, in effect, "What Margaret Murray has theorized is quite true. Witchcraft *was* a religion and, in fact, still is. I am a Witch myself." He went on to tell how the Craft was still very much alive, though underground. He explained, so far as he was allowed, just what Witches did and what they believed; as opposed to what—thanks to the Church's lengthy propaganda—it was generally thought that they did and believed. Since Wica is a Mystery Religion, similar to the old Greek and Roman ones, with an oath of secrecy taken at the Initiation, Gardner was not able to tell everything. But he certainly told a great deal, and enough to show what nonsense was the "information" previously obtainable.

At the time of Gardner's writing it seemed, to him, that the Craft was only just alive. He was greatly surprised when, as a result of the circulation of his books, he began to hear from many covens in all parts of Europe still happily practicing their beliefs. It is now known that there are covens in England, Scotland, Wales, Ireland, Isle of Man, France, Belgium, Holland, Germany, Spain, Italy, South

---

\* *Witchcraft Today* is the classic book on the Craft for anyone at all interested in the subject.

Africa, Australia, New Zealand, Japan, Iceland, Russia, United States . . . virtually around the world.

In only recent years did the Craft surface in America. This is understandable when it is considered that the time this country was first populated was the time of the fierce persecutions of the Witches in Europe. One or two individual Witches may have come here but it seems doubtful that complete covens did. The individual Wican family may have died out, so there is no long background of true Witchcraft in the United States. As of the time of writing* there are now covens in New York, New Jersey, Kentucky, California, Washington D.C., Ohio, and in Ontario, Canada. All of these covens are descended, through the New York one, from the coven to which Dr. Gerald Gardner belonged.

---

\* 1966

# Bibliography

Allen, J. R. and Anderson, J. *The Early Christian Monuments of Scotland*. Edinburgh, 1903.

Anderson, A. O. *Early Sources of Scottish History* (2 vols). Edinburgh, 1922.

Anwyl, Edward. *Celtic Religion in Pre-Christian Times*. London, 1906.

Bolton, Brett L. *The Secret Power of Plants*. New York, 1974.

Bord, Janet and Colin. *Earth Rites*. London, 1982.

Bowra, C. M. *Primitive Song*.

Buckland, Raymond. *Buckland's Complete Book of Witchcraft*. St. Paul, 1986.

_____. *Practical Color Magick*. St. Paul, 1983.

_____. *Secrets Of Gypsy Love Magick*. St. Paul, 1990.

Buckland, Tara. *How to Make an Easy Charm to Attract Love into Your Life*. St. Paul, 1990.

Campbell, J. G. *Witchcraft and Second Sight in the Highlands and Islands of Scotland*. Edinburgh, 1902.

Carmichael, Alexander. *Carmina Gadelica—The Sun Dances*. Edinburgh, 1977.

Chadwick, H. M. *Early Scotland*. Cambridge, 1949.

Childe, V. Gordon. *Scotland Before the Scots*. London, 1946.

Cunningham, Scott. *Wicca—A Guide for the Solitary Practitioner*. St. Paul, 1988.

_____. *Earth Power*. St. Paul, 1983.

Dalyell, J. G. *Darker Superstitions of Scotland*. Edinburgh, 1834.

Davidson, Thomas. *Rowan Tree and Red Thread*. Edinburgh, 1949.

Douglas, R. MacDonald. *The Scots Book of Lore and Folklore*. New York, 1982.

Eliade, Mercia. *Patterns in Comparative Religion.*. New York, 1958.

Fernald, M. L. and Kinsey, A. C. *Edible Wild Plants of Eastern North America.*. New York, 1958.

Frazer, Sir James. *The Golden Bough.*. London, 1890.

_____. *The Worship of Nature*. London, 1926.

Gibbons, Euell. *Stalking the Healthful Herbs*. New York, 1966.

Harrington, H. D. *Edible Native Plants of the Rocky Mountains*. Albuquerque, 1967.

Hubert, H. *The Rise of the Celts*. London, 1934.

Jackson, Kenneth. *A Celtic Miscellany*. London, 1971.

Keator, Glen. *Pacific Coast Berry Finder*. (Pocket Manual), Berkeley, 1978.

Kennedy, D. *England's Dances*. London, 1949.

Kingsbury, John M. *Poisonous Plants of the United States and Canada*. New Jersey, 1964.

Kirk, Donald R. *Wild Edible Plants of Western North America*. 1975.

Lucas, R. *Herbs For Healthful Living*. New York, 1969.

Lust, John. *The Herb Book*. New York, 1974. [Note: If you have only one herbal, let it be this one!]

MacAlpine, Neil. *Pronouncing Gaelic-English Dictionary*. Glasgow, 1973.

MacBain, A. *The Highlanders of Scotland*. London, 1836.

Mackenzie, Alexander. *The Prophesies of the Brahan Seer*. Inverness, 1882.

Maule, Henry and Sibbald, Sir Robert. *The History Of The Picts*. Glasgow, 1818.

McNeill, F. Marian. *The Silver Bough* (4 vols). Glasgow, 1956.

_____. *The Scots Kitchen*, London, 1929.

_____. *The Scots Cellar*, London, 1973.

McPherson, J. M. *Primitive Beliefs in the North-east of Scotland*. London, 1929.

Medsger, Oliver P. *Edible Wild Plants*. New York, 1939.

Meyer, J. E. *The Herbalist*. Indiana, 1971.

Nature Study Guild: *Berry Finder*. Berkeley, CA .

_____. *Track Finder*. Berkeley, CA.

Rust, James. *Druidism Exhumed*. London, 1871.

Spence, Lewis. *Encyclopedia of the Occult*. London, 1920.

_____. *The Magic Arts of Celtic Britain*. London, 1946.

_____. *Myth and Ritual in Dance, Game and Rhyme*. London, 1947.

Stevens, Jose and Lena. *Secrets of Shamanism*. New York, 1988.

Strutt, J. *Sports and Pastimes of the People of England*. London, 1845.

Swire, Otta F. *The Outer Hebrides and Their Legends*. Edinburgh, 1966.

Tompkins, P. and Bird, C. *The Secret Life of Plants*. New York, 1973.

Treben, Maria. *Health Through God's Pharmacy*. Steyr (Austria), 1982.

Wainwright, F. T. (Ed.) *The Problem of the Picts*. Perth, 1980.

Watson, W. J. *Celtic Placenames of Scotland*. Edinburgh nd.

Westwood, Jennifer. *Albion*. London, 1985.

Whitlock, Ralph. *In Search of Lost Gods*. London, 1979.

Zimmer, H. *Matriarchy Among the Picts*. Edinburgh, 1898

**Recordings** (which include rhythmic drumming, etc.)

"Thunderdrums" – Scott Fitzgerald, Nature Recordings No. XXII, Friday Harbor, WA, 1989

"Totem", "Initiation" and "Bones" – Gabrielle Roth and The Mirrors, The Moving Center, Red Bank, NJ, 1988.

"Earth Tribe Rhythms" – Brent Lewis Productions, Los Angeles, CA, 1990.

"Miriam Makeba: Sangoma" – Warner Bros. Records, 1988 (also available on C.D.).

Any good Scottish reels.

# STAY IN TOUCH

On the following pages you will find listed, with their current prices, some of the books and tapes now available on related subjects. Your book dealer stocks most of these, and will stock new titles in the Llewellyn series as they become available. We urge your patronage.

To obtain our full catalog, to keep informed of new titles as they are released and to benefit from informative articles and helpful news, write for our bi-monthly news magazine/catalog. A sample copy is free, and it will continue coming to you at no cost as long as you are an active mail customer. Or keep it coming for a full year with a donation of just $5.00 in U.S.A. and Canada ($20.00 overseas, first class mail). Many bookstores also have *The Llewellyn New Times* available. Ask for it.

Stay in touch! In *The Llewellyn New Times'* pages you will find news and reviews of new books, tapes and services, announcements of meetings and seminars, helpful articles, news of authors, advertising of products and services, special money-making opportunities, and much more.

### *The Llewellyn New Times*
### P.O. Box 64383-Dept. 057, St. Paul, MN 55164-0383, U.S.A.

• • •

# TO ORDER BOOKS AND TAPES

If your book dealer does not have the books and tapes described on the following pages readily available, you may order them directly from the publisher by sending full price in U.S. funds, plus $1.50 for postage and handling for orders *under* $10.00; $3.00 for orders *over* $10.00. There are no postage and handling charges for orders over $50. UPS Delivery: We ship UPS whenever possible. Delivery guaranteed. Provide your street address as UPS does not deliver to P.O. Boxes. UPS to Canada requires a $50 minimum order. Allow 4-6 weeks for delivery. Orders outside the U.S.A. and Canada: Airmail—add retail price of book; add $5 for each non-book item (tapes, etc.); add $1 per item for surface mail.

# FOR GROUP STUDY AND PURCHASE

Because there is a great deal of interest in group discussion and study of the subject matter of this book, we encourage use of the book by such groups by offering a special quantity price to group leaders or agents.

Our Special Quantity Price for a minimum order of five copies of *Scottish Witchcraft* is $29.85 cash-with-order. This price includes postage and handling within the United States. Minnesota residents must add 6.5% sales tax. For additional quantities, please order in multiples of five. For Canadian and foreign orders, add postage and handling charges as above. Credit card (VISA, Master Card, American Express) orders are accepted. Charge card orders only may be phoned free ($15.00 minimum order) within the U.S.A. or Canada by dialing 1-800-THE-MOON. Customer service calls dial 1-612-291-1970. Mail Orders to:

### LLEWELLYN PUBLICATIONS
### P.O. Box 64383-Dept. 057 / St. Paul, MN 55164-0383, U.S.A.

Prices subject to change.

## SECRETS OF GYPSY DREAM READING
### by Raymond Buckland, Ph.D.

The Gypsies have carried their arcane wisdom and time-tested methods of dream interpretation around the world. Now, in *Secrets of Gypsy Dream Reading*, Raymond Buckland, a descendant of the Romani Gypsies, reveals these fascinating methods.

Learn how to accurately interpret dreams, dream the future, dream for profit, remember your dreams more clearly, and willfully direct your dreams. The Gypsies' observations on dreaming are extremely perceptive and enlightening. They say that dreams are messages, giving advice on what is most beneficial for you. Many times these messages could mean the difference between happiness and misery—if not life and death.

In today's fast-paced, often superficial world, we need to listen to the Gypsies' words of wisdom more than ever. Listen to your dreams and achieve success, riches, better health—and more—in your waking hours!

**0-87542-086-9, 220 pgs., mass market, illus.**                 **$3.95**


## BUCKLAND'S COMPLETE BOOK OF WITCHCRAFT
### by Raymond Buckland, Ph.D.

Here is the most complete resource to the study and practice of modern, non-denominational Wicca. This is a lavishly illustrated, self-study course for the solitary or group. Included are rituals, exercises for developing psychic talents, and information on all major "sects" of the Craft, sections on tools, beliefs, dreams, meditations, divination, herbal lore, healing, ritual clothing and much, much more. This book unites theory and practice into a comprehensive course designed to help you develop into a practicing Witch, one of the "Wise Ones." It is written by Dr. Ray Buckland, a very famous and respected authority on witchcraft who first came public with "the Old Religion" in the United States. Large format with workbook-type exercises, profusely illustrated and full of music and chants. Takes you from A to Z in the study of Witchcraft.

Never before has so much information on "the Craft of the Wise" been collected in one place. Traditionally, there are three degrees of advancement in most Wiccan traditions. When you complete studying this book you will be the equivalent of a "Third Degree Witch." Even those who have practiced Wicca for years find useful information in this book, and many covens are using this for their textbook. If you want to become a Witch, or if you merely want to find out what Witchcraft is really about, you will find no better book than this.

**0-87542-050-8, 272 pgs., 8 1/2 x 11, illus., softcover**            **$14.95**

## PRACTICAL CANDLEBURNING RITUALS
### by Raymond Buckland, Ph. D.

Another book in Llewellyn's Practical Magick series. Magick is a way in which to apply the full range of your hidden psychic powers to the problems we all face in daily life. We know that normally we use only 5% of our total powers—Magick taps powers from deep inside our psyche where we are in contact with the Universe's limitless resources.

Magick need not be complex—it can be as simple as using a few candles to focus your mind, a simple ritual to give direction to your desire, a few words to give expression to your wish.

This book shows you how easy it can be. Here is Magick for fun, Magick as a Craft, Magick for Success, Love, Luck, Money, Marriage, Healing; Magick to stop slander, to learn truth, to heal an unhappy marriage, to overcome a bad habit, to break up love affair, etc.

Magick—with nothing fancier than ordinary candles, and the 28 rituals in this book (given in both Christian and Old Religion versions)—can transform your life. Illustrated.

0–87542–048–06, 189 pgs., 5 1/4 x 8, softcover                    $6.95

## PRACTICAL COLOR MAGICK
### by Raymond Buckland

The world is a rainbow of color, a symphony of vibration. We have left the Newtonian idea of the world as being made of large mechanical units, and now know it as a strange chaos of vibrations ordered by our senses, but our senses are limited and designed by Nature to give us access to only those vibratory emanations we need for survival.

But, we live far from the natural world now. And the colors which filled our habitats when we were natural creatures have given way to gray and black and synthetic colors of limited wavelengths determined not by our physiological needs but by economic constraints.

Learn the secret meanings of color; use color to change the energy centers of your body, heal yourself and others through light radiction, and discover the hidden aspects of your personality through color.

This book will teach all the powers of light and more. You'll learn new forms of expression of your innermost self, new ways of relating to others with the secret languages of light and color. Put true color back into your life with the rich spectrum of ideas and practical magical formulas from *Practical Color Magick!*

0–87542–047–6, 136 pgs., illus., softcover                    $6.95

## HOW TO MAKE AN EASY CHARM
## TO ATTRACT LOVE INTO YOUR LIFE
**by Tara Buckland**

Everyone wants a happy love life. In today's world, singles organizations thrive on this fact, as divorce and increased personal independence create more love-hungry people than ever before. In this book, Tara Buckland presents an introduction to magick, a quiz for the person seeking love, Egyptian love spells, and techniques for building an Egyptian love amulet.

Buckland, an authority on Egyptian magick, explains the importance of magick in the ancient land, how the relatively unattractive Cleopatra used it to attract many lovers, and how the Egyptians' ancient knowledge is especially pertinent today.

**0-87542-087-7, mass market, illus.** $3.95

## SECRETS OF GYPSY FORTUNETELLING
**by Ray Buckland**

This book unveils the Romani secrets of fortune-telling, explaining in detail the many different methods used by these nomads. For generations they have survived on their skills as seers. Their accuracy is legendary. They are a people who seem to be born with "the sight"... the ability to look into the past, present and future using only the simplest of tools to aid them. Here you will learn to read palms, to interpret the symbols in a teacup, to read cards... both the Tarot and regular playing cards. Here are revealed the secrets of interpreting the actions of animals, of reading the weather, of recognizing birthmarks and the shape of hands. Impress your friends with your knowledge of many of these lesser Mysteries; uncommon forms of fortune-telling known only to a few.

The methods of divination presented in this book are all practical methods—no expensive or hard-to-get items are necessary. The Gypsies are accomplished at using natural objects and everyday items to serve them in their endeavors. Sticks and stones, knives and needles, cards and dice... some are found along the roadside, or in the woods, others are easily obtainable at little expense from the five-and-dime, the convenience store, or the traveling peddler. Using these non-complex objects, and following the traditional Gypsy ways shown, you can become a seer and improve the quality of your own life and of these lives around you.

**ISBN: 0-87542-051-6, mass market, 220 pgs., illus.** $3.95